CLEAN WATER ACT:
CURRENT ISSUES AND GUIDE TO BOOKS

CLEAN WATER ACT:
CURRENT ISSUES AND GUIDE TO BOOKS

CLAUDIA COPELAND

Nova Science Publishers, Inc.
New York

Senior Editors: Susan Boriotti and Donna Dennis
Coordinating Editor: Tatiana Shohov
Office Manager: Annette Hellinger
Graphics: Wanda Serrano
Editorial Production: Maya Columbus, Vladimir Klestov, Matthew Kozlowski, Tom Moceri and Anthony T. Sovak
Circulation: Ave Maria Gonzalez, Vera Popovic, Luis Aviles, Raymond Davis, Melissa Diaz, Magdalene Nunez, Marlene Nunez and Jeannie Pappas
Communications and Acquisitions: Serge P. Shohov
Marketing: Cathy DeGregory

Library of Congress Cataloging-in-Publication Data
Available Upon Request

Ref
KF
3790
.C67x
2003

ISBN: 1-59033-618-6.

Copyright © 2003 by Nova Science Publishers, Inc.
400 Oser Ave, Suite 1600
Hauppauge, New York 11788-3619
Tele. 631-231-7269   Fax 631-231-8175
e-mail: Novascience@earthlink.net
Web Site: http://www.novapublishers.com

Printed in the United States of America

CONTENTS

PREFACE

The Clean Water Act (CWA) requires states to identify waters that are impaired by pollution, even after application of pollution controls. For these waters, states must establish a total maximum daily load (TMDL) of pollutants to ensure that water quality standards can be attained. Implementation was dormant until states and the Environmental Protection Agency (EPA) were prodded by numerous lawsuits. The TMDL program has become controversial, in part because eof requirements and costs now facing states to implement this 30-year old provision of the law. In 1999, EPA proposed regulatory changes to strengthen the TMDL program. Industries, cities farmers and others may be required to use new pollution controls to meet TMDL requirements. EPA's proposal was widely criticized and congressional interest has been high.

This book explores the lingering dispute between states and industry groups, beginning from the Clinton administration and stretching all the way to the present. However, Congress recognized in the Act that, in many cases, pollution controls implemented by industry and cities would be insufficient, due to pollutant contributions from other unregulated sources.

Chapter 1

CLEAN WATER ACT:
A SUMMARY OF THE LAW

INTRODUCTION

The principal law governing pollution of the nation's surface waters is the Federal Water Pollution Control Act, or Clean Water Act. Originally enacted in 1948, it was totally revised by amendments in 1972 that gave the Act its current shape. The 1972 legislation spelled out ambitious programs for water quality improvement that have since been expanded and are still being implemented by industries and municipalities. Congress made certain fine-tuning amendments in 1977, revised portions of the law in 1981, and enacted further amendments in 1987.

This chapter presents a summary of the law, describing the essence of the statute. Many details and secondary provisions are omitted here, and even some major components are only briefly mentioned. Further, this chapter describes the statute without discussing its implementation. Table 1 shows the original enactment and subsequent major amendments. Table 2, at the end of this chapter, cites the major U.S. Code sections of the codified statute.

Table 1. Clean Water Act and Major Amendments
(codified generally as 33 U.S.C. 1251-1387)

Year	Act	Public Law
1948	Federal Water Pollution Control Act	P.L. 80-845 (Act of June 30, 1948)
1956	Water Pollution Control Act of 1956	P.L. 84-660 (Act of July 9, 1956)
1961	Federal Water Pollution Control Act Amendments	P.L. 87-88
1965	Water Quality Act of 1965	P.L. 89-234
1966	Clean Water Restoration Act	P.L. 89-753
1970	Water Quality Improvement Act of 1970	P.L. 91-224, Part I
1972	Federal Water Pollution Control Act Amendments	P.L. 92-500
1977	Clean Water Act of 1977	P.L. 95-217
1981	Municipal Wastewater Treatment Construction Grants Amendments	P.L. 97-117
1987	Water Quality Act of 1987	P.L. 100-4

Authorizations for appropriations to support the law generally expired at the end of fiscal year 1990 (Sept. 30, 1990). Programs did not lapse, however, and Congress has continued to appropriate funds to carry out the Act. Since the 1987 amendments, although Congress has enacted several bills that reauthorize and modify a number of individual provisions in the law, none comprehensively addressed major programs or requirements.

BACKGROUND

The Federal Water Pollution Control Act of 1948 was the first comprehensive statement of federal interest in clean water programs, and it specifically provided state and local governments with technical assistance funds to address water pollution problems, including research. Water pollution was viewed as primarily a state and local problem, hence, there were no federally required goals, objectives, limits, or even guidelines. When it came to enforcement, federal involvement was strictly limited to matters involving interstate waters and only with the consent of the state in which the pollution originated.

During the latter half of the 1950s and well into the 1960s, water pollution control programs were shaped by four laws which amended the 1948 statute. They dealt largely with federal assistance to municipal dischargers and with federal enforcement programs for all dischargers. During this period, the federal role and federal jurisdiction were gradually extended to include navigable intrastate, as well as interstate, waters. Water quality standards became a feature of the law in 1965, requiring states to set standards for interstate waters that would be used to determine actual pollution levels and control requirements. By the late 1960s, there was a widespread perception that existing enforcement procedures were too time-consuming and that the water quality standards approach was flawed because of difficulties in linking a particular discharger to violations of stream quality standards. Additionally, there was mounting frustration over the slow pace of pollution cleanup efforts and a suspicion that control technologies were being developed but not applied to the problems. These perceptions and frustrations, along with increased public interest in environmental protection, set the stage for the 1972 amendments.

The 1972 statute did not continue the basic components of previous laws as much as it set up new ones. It set optimistic and ambitious goals, required all municipal and industrial wastewater to be treated before being discharged into waterways, increased federal assistance for municipal treatment plant construction, strengthened and streamlined enforcement, and expanded the federal role while retaining the responsibility of states for day-to-day implementation of the law.

The 1972 legislation declared as its objective the restoration and maintenance of the chemical, physical, and biological integrity of the nation's waters. Two goals also were established: zero discharge of pollutants by 1985 and, as an interim goal and where possible, water quality that is both "fishable" and "swimmable" by mid-1983. While those dates have passed, the goals remain, and efforts to attain them continue.

OVERVIEW

The Clean Water Act (CWA) today consists of two major parts, one being the title II and title VI provisions which authorize federal financial assistance for municipal sewage treatment plant construction. The other is the regulatory requirements, found throughout the Act, that apply to industrial and municipal dischargers.

The Act has been termed a technology-forcing statute because of the rigorous demands placed on those who are regulated by it to achieve higher and higher levels of pollution abatement. Industries were given until July 1, 1977, to install "best practicable control technology" (BPT) to clean up waste discharges. Municipal wastewater treatment plants were required to meet an equivalent goal, termed "secondary treatment," by that date. (Municipalities unable to achieve secondary treatment by that date were allowed to apply for case-by-case extensions up to July 1, 1988. According to EPA, 86% of all cities met the 1988 deadline; the remainder were put under judicial or administrative schedules requiring compliance as soon as possible. However, many cities, especially smaller ones, continue to make investments in building or upgrading facilities needed to achieve secondary treatment.) Cities that discharge wastes into marine waters were eligible for case-by-case waivers of the secondary treatment requirement, where sufficient showing could be made that natural factors provide significant elimination of traditional forms of pollution and that both balanced populations of fish, shellfish, and wildlife and water quality standards would be protected.

The primary focus of BPT was on controlling discharges of conventional pollutants, such as suspended solids, biochemical oxygen demanding materials, fecal coliform and bacteria, and pH. These pollutants are substances which are biodegradable (i.e., bacteria can break them down), occur naturally in the aquatic environment, and deplete the dissolved oxygen concentration in water which is necessary for fish and other aquatic life.

The Act required greater pollutant cleanup than BPT by no later than March 31, 1989, generally demanding that industry use the "best available technology" (BAT) that is economically achievable. BAT level controls generally focus on toxic substances. Compliance extensions of as long as 2 years are available for industrial sources utilizing innovative or alternative technology. Failure to meet statutory deadlines could lead to enforcement action.

The Act utilizes both water quality standards and technology-based effluent limitations to protect water quality. Technology-based effluent limitations are specific numerical limitations established by EPA and placed on certain pollutants from certain sources. They are applied to industrial and municipal sources through numerical effluent limitations in discharge permits (see discussion of Permits, Regulation, and Enforcement, below). Water quality standards are standards for the overall quality of water. They consist of the designated beneficial use or uses of a waterbody (recreation, water supply, industrial, or other), plus a numerical or narrative statement identifying maximum concentrations of various pollutants which would not interfere with the designated use. The Act requires each state to establish water quality standards for all bodies of water in the state. These standards serve as the backup to federally set technology-based requirements by indicating where additional pollutant controls are needed to achieve the overall goals of the Act. In waters where industrial and municipal sources have achieved technology-based effluent limitations, yet water quality standards have not been met, dischargers may be required to meet additional pollution control requirements.

Control of toxic pollutant discharges has been a key focus of water quality programs. In addition to the BPT and BAT national standards, states are required to implement control strategies for waters expected to remain polluted by toxic chemicals even after industrial dischargers have installed the best available cleanup technologies required under the law. Development of management programs for these post-BAT pollutant problems was a prominent element in the 1987 amendments and is a key continuing aspect of CWA implementation.

Prior to the 1987 amendments, programs in the Clean Water Act were primarily directed at point source pollution, wastes discharged from discrete and identifiable sources, such as pipes and other outfalls. In contrast, except for general planning activities, little attention had been given to nonpoint source pollution (stormwater runoff from agricultural lands, forests, construction sites, and urban areas), despite estimates that it represents more than 50% of the nation's remaining water pollution problems. As it travels across land surface towards rivers and streams, rainfall and snowmelt runoff picks up pollutants, including sediments, toxic materials, and conventional wastes (e.g., nutrients) that can degrade water quality.

The 1987 amendments authorized measures to address such pollution by directing states to develop and implement nonpoint pollution management programs (section 319 of the Act). States were encouraged to pursue groundwater protection activities as part of their overall nonpoint pollution control efforts. Federal financial assistance was authorized to support demonstration projects and actual control activities. These grants may cover up to 60% of program implementation costs.

While the Act imposes great technological demands, it also recognizes the need for comprehensive research on water quality problems. This is provided throughout the statute, on topics including pollution in the Great Lakes and Chesapeake Bay, in-place toxic pollutants in harbors and navigable waterways, and water pollution resulting from mine drainage. The Act also provides support to train personnel who operate and maintain wastewater treatment facilities.

Federal and State Responsibilities

Under this Act, federal jurisdiction is broad, particularly regarding establishment of national standards or effluent limitations. The Environmental Protection Agency (EPA) issues regulations containing the BPT and BAT effluent standards applicable to categories of industrial sources (such as iron and steel manufacturing, organic chemical manufacturing, petroleum refining, and others). Certain responsibilities are delegated to the states, and this Act, like other environmental laws, embodies a philosophy of federal-state partnership in which the federal government sets the agenda and standards for pollution abatement, while states carry out day-to-day activities of implementation and enforcement. Delegated responsibilities under the Act include authority for qualified states to issue discharge permits to industries and municipalities and to enforce permits. (As of January 2002, 45 states had been delegated responsibility for this permit program; EPA issues discharge permits in the remaining states.)

In addition, as noted above, states are responsible for establishing water quality standards.

TITLES II AND VI — MUNICIPAL WASTEWATER TREATMENT CONSTRUCTION

Federal law has authorized grants for planning, design, and construction of municipal sewage treatment facilities since 1956 (Act of July 9, 1956, or P.L. 84-660). Congress greatly expanded this grant is program in 1972 in order to assist cities in meeting the Act's pollution control requirements. Since that time Congress has authorized $65 billion and appropriated $73 billion in funds to aid wastewater treatment plant construction. Grants are allocated among the states according to a complex statutory formula that combines two factors: state population and an estimate of municipal sewage treatment funding needs derived from a biennial survey conducted by EPA and the states. The most recent estimate, completed in 1996, indicates that $140 billion more would be required to build and upgrade needed municipal wastewater treatment plants in the United States and for other types of water quality improvement projects that are eligible for funding under the Act.

Under the title II construction grants program established in 1972, federal grants were made for several types of projects (such as secondary or more stringent treatment and associated sewers) based on a priority list established by the states. Grants were generally available for as much as 55% of total project costs. For projects using innovative or alternative technology (such as reuse or recycling of water), as much as 75% federal funding was allowed. Recipients were responsible for non-federal costs but were not required to repay federal grants.

Policymakers have debated the tension between assisting municipal funding needs, which remain large, and the impact of aid programs such as the Clean Water Act's on federal spending and budget deficits. In the 1987 amendments to the Act, Congress attempted to deal with that apparent conflict by extending federal aid for wastewater treatment construction through fiscal year 1994, yet providing a transition towards full state and local government responsibility for financing after that date. Grants under the traditional title II program were authorized through fiscal year 1990. Under title VI of the Act, grants to capitalize State Water Pollution Control Revolving Funds, or loan programs, were authorized beginning in fiscal year 1989 to replace the title II grants. States contribute matching funds, and under the revolving loan fund concept, monies used for wastewater treatment construction will be repaid to a state fund, to be available for future construction in other communities. All states now have functioning loan programs, but the shift from federal grants to loans, since fiscal year 1991, has been easier for some than others. The new financing requirements have been a problem for cities (especially small towns) that have difficulty repaying project loans. Statutory authorization for grants to capitalize state loan programs expired in 1994; however, Congress has continued to provide annual appropriations. An issue affecting some cities is overflow discharges of inadequately treated wastes from municipal sewers and how cities will pay for costly remediation projects. In 2000, Congress amended the Act to authorize a $1.5 billion grant program to help cities reduce these wet weather flows.

PERMITS, REGULATIONS, AND ENFORCEMENT

To achieve its objectives, the Act embodies the concept that all discharges into the nation's waters are unlawful, unless specifically authorized by a permit. Thus, more than 65,000 industrial and municipal dischargers must obtain permits from EPA (or qualified states) under the Act's National Pollutant Discharge Elimination System (NPDES) program (authorized in section 402 of the Act). An NPDES permit requires the discharger (source) to attain technology-based effluent limits (BPT or BAT for industry, secondary treatment for municipalities, or more stringent for water quality protection). Permits specify the control technology applicable to each pollutant, the effluent limitations a discharger must meet, and the deadline for compliance. Sources are required to maintain records and to carry out effluent monitoring activities. Permits are issued for 5-year periods and must be renewed thereafter to allow continued discharge.

The NPDES permit incorporates numerical effluent limitations issued by EPA. The initial BPT limitations focused on regulating discharges of conventional pollutants, such as bacteria and oxygen-consuming materials. The more stringent BAT limitations emphasize controlling toxic pollutants — heavy metals, pesticides, and other organic chemicals. In addition to these limitations applicable to categories of industry, EPA has issued water quality criteria for more than 115 pollutants, including 65 named classes or categories of toxic chemicals, or "priority pollutants." These criteria recommend ambient, or overall, concentration levels for the pollutants and provide guidance to states for establishing water quality standards that will achieve the goals of the Act.

A separate type of permit is required to dispose of dredge or fill material in the nation's waters, including wetlands. Authorized by section 404 of the Act, this permit program is administered by the U.S. Army Corps of Engineers, subject to and using EPA's environmental guidance. Some types of activities are exempt from permit requirements, including certain farming, ranching, and forestry practices which do not alter the use or character of the land; some construction and maintenance; and activities already regulated by states under other provisions of the Act. EPA may delegate certain section 404 permitting responsibility to qualified states and has done so twice (Michigan and New Jersey). For some time, the Act's wetlands permit program has become one of the most controversial parts of the law. Some who wish to develop wetlands maintain that federal regulation intrudes on and impedes private land-use decisions, while environmentalists seek more protection for remaining wetlands and limits on activities that take place in wetlands.

Nonpoint sources of pollution, which EPA and states believe are responsible for the majority of water quality impairments in the nation, are not subject to CWA permits or other regulatory requirements under federal law. They are covered by state programs for the management of runoff, under section 319 of the Act.

Other EPA regulations under the CWA include guidelines on using and disposing of sewage sludge and guidelines for discharging pollutants from land-based sources into the ocean. (A related statute, the Ocean Dumping Act, regulates the intentional disposal of wastes into ocean waters.) EPA also provides guidance on technologies that will achieve BPT, BAT, and other effluent limitations.

The NPDES permit, containing effluent limitations on what may be discharged by a source, is the Act's principal enforcement tool. EPA may issue a compliance order or bring a civil suit in U.S. district court against persons who violate the terms of a permit. The penalty for such a violation can be as much as $25,000 per day. Stiffer penalties are authorized for criminal violations of the Act — for negligent or knowing violations — of as much as $50,000 per day, 3 years' imprisonment, or both. A fine of as much as $250,000, 15 years in prison, or both, is authorized for 'knowing endangerment' — violations that knowingly place another person in imminent danger of death or serious bodily injury. Finally, EPA is authorized to assess civil penalties administratively for certain well-documented violations of the law. These civil and criminal enforcement provisions are contained in section 309 of the Act. EPA, working with the Army Corps of Engineers, also has responsibility for enforcing against entities who engage in activities that destroy or alter wetlands.

While the CWA addresses federal enforcement, the majority of actions taken to enforce the law are undertaken by states, both because states issue the majority of permits to dischargers and because the federal government lacks the resources for day-to-day monitoring and enforcement. Like most other federal environmental laws, CWA enforcement is shared by EPA and states, with states having primary responsibility. However, EPA has oversight of state enforcement and retains the right to bring a direct action where it believes that a state has failed to take timely and appropriate action or where a state or local agency requests EPA involvement. Finally, the federal government acts to enforce against criminal violations of the federal law.

In addition, individuals may bring a citizen suit in U.S. district court against persons who violate a prescribed effluent standard or limitation. Individuals also may bring citizen suits against the Administrator of EPA or equivalent state official (where program responsibility has been delegated to the state) for failure to carry out a nondiscretionary duty under the Act.

SELECTED REFERENCES

Loeb, Penny. *Very Troubled Waters*. U.S. NEWS & WORLD REPORT, vol. 125, no. 12. Sept. 28, 1998. pp. 39, 41-42.

Schneider, Paul. *Clear Progress, 25 Years of the Clean Water Act*. AUDUBON. September/October 1997. pp. 36-47, 106-107.

U.S. Environmental Protection Agency. Office of Water. *Environmental Indicators of Water Quality in the United States*. EPA 841-R-96-002. June 1996. 30 p.

—— *The Quality of Our Nation's Water: 1998 Report to Congress*. Washington, June 2000. EPA841-R-00-001. 413 p.

U.S. General Accounting Office. *Key EPA and State Decisions Limited by Inconsistent and Incomplete Data*. GAO/RCED-00-54. March 2000. 73 p.

—— *Water Quality, A Catalog of Related Federal Programs*. GAO/RCED-96-173. 64 p.

Table 2. Major U.S. Code Sectons of the Clean Water Act[1]
(codified generally as 33 U.S.C. 1251-1387)

33 U.S.C.	Section Title	Clean Water Act (as amended)
Subchapter I -	Research and Related Programs	
1251	Congressional declaration of goals and policy	sec. 101
1252	Comprehensive programs for water pollution control	sec. 102
1253	Interstate cooperation and uniform laws	sec. 103
1254	Research, investigations, training and information	sec. 104
1255	Grants for research and development	sec. 105
1256	Grants for pollution control programs	sec. 106
1257	Mine water pollution demonstrations	sec. 107
1258	Pollution control in the Great Lakes	sec. 108
1259	Training grants and contracts	sec. 109
1260	Applications for training grants and contracts, allocations	sec. 110
1261	Scholarships	sec. 111
1262	Definitions and authorization	sec. 112
1263	Alaska village demonstration project	sec. 113
1265	In-place toxic pollutants	sec. 115
1266	Hudson River reclamation demonstration project	sec. 116
1267	Chesapeake Bay	sec. 117
1268	Great Lakes	sec. 118
1269	Long Island Sound	sec. 119
1270	Lake Champlain management conference	sec. 120

[1] NOTE: This table shows only the major code sections. For more detail and to determine when a section was added, the reader should consult the official printed version of the U.S. Code.

Chapter 2

CLEAN WATER ACT SECTION 401: BACKGROUND AND ISSUES

INTRODUCTION

Section 401 of the Clean Water Act requires that an applicant for a federal license or permit provide a certification that any discharges from a facility will comply with the Act, including water quality standard requirements. Disputes have arisen over the states' exercise of authority under Section 401. Until recently, much of the debate over the Section 401 certification issue has been between states and hydropower interests. A 1994 Supreme Court decision which upheld the states' authority in this area dismayed development and hydroelectric power interest groups. The dispute between states and industry groups was a legislative issue in the 104th Congress through a provision of a House-passed Clean Water Act reauthorization bill; the Senate did not act on that bill. There was no similar activity in the 105th or 106th Congress. It could be an issue in the 107th Congress in the context of energy policy debate and reforming hydropower licensing proceedings. In addition, interest could develop in clarifying whether Section 401 certification applies to nonpoint source pollution discharges, as well as point sources. This question was raised in an Oregon lawsuit; the court ruled that Section 401 does not apply to nonpoint source discharges. This report will be updated as warranted.

BACKGROUND

Under provisions of the Clean Water Act (CWA), an applicant for a federal license or permit to conduct any activity that may result in a discharge to navigable waters must provide the federal agency with a Section 401 certification. The certification, made by the state in which the discharge originates, declares that the discharge will comply with applicable provisions of the Act, including water quality standards requirements.

Section 401 provides states with two distinct powers: one, the power indirectly to deny federal permits or licenses by withholding certification; and two, the power to impose conditions upon federal permits by placing limitations on certification. Generally, Section 401 certification has been applied to hydroelectric projects seeking a license from the Federal Energy Regulatory Commission (FERC) and for dredge-and-fill activities in wetlands and other waters that require permits from the Army Corps of Engineers under Section 404 of the CWA and Sections 9 and 10 of the Rivers and Harbors Act It also is applied to permit requirements for industrial and municipal point source dischargers under Section 402 of the CWA. In addition, it has the potential to be applied to a range of other activities that could affect water quality, a point that has increasingly become an issue.

Because participation by states in Section 401 certification is optional (they may waive the authority if they choose to do so), state implementation has varied. In recent years, however, some states have come to view Section 401 as an important tool in their overall programs to protect the physical and biological, in addition to the chemical, integrity of their waters. Some have begun using Section 401 to address a wide range of impacts to the quality of their waters, including impacts to aquatic habitat such as wetlands where issues of non-chemical impacts arise. Through Section 401, some states have addressed such impacts of a project as inadequate river flow, inundation of habitat, dissolved oxygen levels, and impacts on fish and other wildlife.

This expanded use of Section 401 has, in turn, led to tensions between state and federal agencies (especially FERC) over the scope of the states' Section 401 authority, particularly the extent to which states can legally address water flow requirements in water quality standards. Some state courts have placed limitations on the use of Section 401 authority (at least for hydropower projects) to address only chemical impacts of projects (such as dissolved oxygen or numeric chemical criteria) and not physical impacts (filling of aquatic habitat in a streambed as a result of the project) or biological impacts (effects on fish migration, for example). Other courts have adopted a broader view and allowed states to condition certification on compliance with all applicable water quality-related laws. A1990 Supreme Court case *(California v. FERC,* 495 U.S. 490, known as the Rock Creek Case) addressed the issue of whether hydropower projects must comply with any aspect of state water use law. It held that, with regard to federally licensed hydropower facilities, the Federal Power Act preempts state water use law, including states' comprehensive arrangements for allocating water among competing uses.

CONCERNS AND LEGISLATIVE ISSUES

Until recently, much of the debate over the Section 401 certification issue was between states and hydropower interests. States have favored clarifying the CWA to confirm their broad authority to impose conditions on federally permitted activities (some also favor amending the Federal Power Act to clarify that it does not preempt state regulation of water uses). This position was described hi testimony at a Senate subcommittee hearing in 1991.[1]

> [A]n overly narrow reading of section 401 would deprive the States of the ability to maintain the very beneficial uses that the Clean Water Act was designed to protect. Federal agencies could permit activities that would undermine a State's investment in pollution control efforts and impose a double standard for different activities affecting the same in-stream values. It makes no sense to authorize States to implement Clean Water Act programs designed to protect beneficial uses and yet leave them powerless to prevent a federally permitted activity from impairing those values.
>
> The comprehensive nature of State management of water quality and water quantity means that the States are best situated to determine whether a federally permitted activity will fully protect beneficial uses. The States have lead responsibility for protecting water quality under the Clean Water Act and for administering laws governing allocation of water quantity. Water quality and quantity are inextricably linked; both are essential to maintaining the integrity of the nation's waters.

Hydropower interests favor allowing federal agencies such as FERC to determine what conditions on a project are necessary for protection of water quality or to

---

[1] Strong, Clive J. Statement on behalf of the National Association of Attorneys General, in, U.S. Congress. Senate. Committee on Environment and Public Works. Subcommittee on Environmental Protection. Water Pollution Prevention and Control Act of 1991. Hearings on S. 1081. 102d Congress, 1st session. Washington, U.S. Govt. Print Off., 1991. (S. Hrg. 102-335) p. 805. (Hereinafter, 1991 Senate Hearing)

satisfy other criteria, in light of the important purposes directed by Congress in other laws, specifically the Federal Power Act.[2]

> The current limitation on the role of the States in the [federal hydropower] licensing process is that ultimately the FERC must make the decision balancing the multitude of resource interests affected by the project The expansive reading of Section 401 water quality certification being used in some States crosses this barrier, using this mandatory water quality review to effectively take control of all aspects of the project. ...Expansion of 401 certification places authority for an energy resource in the effective control of a State water quality agency, that is not responsible for utility rate stabilization, assuring adequate water supplies, promoting clean air technology, or controlling floods.

In the 103rd Congress, interest in clarifying the scope of Section 401 certification authority led to several legislative proposals. The Senate Environment and Public Works Committee included a provision in S. 2093, a CWA reauthorization bill (S. Rept. 103-257). S. 2093 would have amended Section 401 to clarify that applicants for a federal license or permit, including applicants for a FERC license to operate hydroelectric generating facilities, must obtain state certification that the project will comply with water quality standards and will allow for attainment and maintenance of designated uses included hi the state's standards. The Senate did not act on S. 2093.

The Supreme Court again considered the Section 401 issue in a case decided after S. 2093 was reported in 1994. *In Public Utility District (PUD) No. 1 of Jefferson County and City of Tacoma* v. *Washington Department of Ecology,* 511 U.S. 700 (1994), the Court held that a state may impose minimum stream flow requirements as a condition hi a Section 401 certification issued for a proposed hydroelectric facility because the CWA allows states to condition certification upon any effluent limitation or other appropriate state law requirement, to ensure that the facility will not violate State water quality standards. Imposition of the condition in question as part of the Section 401 certification did not conflict with FERC's authority to issue a license under the Federal Power Act, the Court said.

This decision supported the position of states, which had sought confirmation of then-power to impose minimum stream flow and other requirements of state water quality standards. Environmentalists, who have supported states' use of Section 401 to address aquatic habitat alteration and biological diversity of the Nation's waters, also were pleased with the ruling. Development and hydropower

---

[2] Greely, Gail Ann. Statement on behalf of the National Hydropower Association, in, 1991 Senate Hearing. P. 810.

interests, on the other hand, were said to be dismayed by the *PUD No. 1* decision, saying that it would make licensing of hydroelectric facilities more difficult and costly, at a time when more than 300 hydro projects are seeking FERC relicensing. Utility industry representatives were said to be concerned that water quality agencies reflect a narrow viewpoint under their mandates and could bias licensing policies by not adequately addressing power needs.

Following the Supreme Court's decision, disputes over Section 401 became an issue in the Congress. At the end of the 103rd Congress, legislation was introduced to amend the Clean Water Act and overturn the *PUD No. 1* decision. The sponsor of the bill, Senator Wallop, said that the decision threatened state water law (by limiting the amount of water that could be used for the project in question and, thus, interfering with state water rights systems) and the integrity of the FERC hydroelectric licensing process (Cong. Rec., daily ed., Nov. 30, 1994, S15237).

The 104th Congress addressed the issue in H.R. 961, a bill to reauthorize the Clean Water Act passed by the House in 1995. Section 507, adopted during House debate, would make Section 401 inapplicable to hydropower projects if FERC determines that the state's certification is inconsistent with the Federal Power Act. The bill also set up a mechanism, to be administered by FERC, to resolve differences that might arise between the state and FERC on questions relating to the consistency of the 401 certification to a hydropower project. That is, in the event of a dispute between FERC and a state over 401 certification of a hydropower project, the federal agency with licensing authority under the Federal Power Act also would oversee resolving the dispute between itself and an individual state.

This amendment to H.R. 961 was one of several proposed to address the issue. Some Members favored simply exempting hydropower projects from Clean Water Act regulation, since FERC project review is intended to consider inputs of state and federal agencies, Indian tribes, and the public in connection with licensing and relicensing decisions. Others argued that states should continue to have authority to regulate matters related to water quality concerns, and the amendment attempted to balance those concerns. No further action occurred on H.R. 961 during the 104th Congress, leaving the issue unresolved. There was no comprehensive legislative action to amend the Clean Water Act during the 105th or 106th Congress.

SECTION 401 AND LAND RUNOFF

In September 1996, a federal district court in Oregon ruled that Section 401 "applies to all federally permitted activities that may result in a discharge, including discharges from nonpoint sources." *(Oregon Natural Desert Association v. Thomas,* 940 F.Supp. 1534, D.Or. 1996) The case, brought by environmental groups in Oregon, sought to have the U.S. Forest Service obtain Section 401 certification from the state that cattle grazing would not violate state water quality standards before issuing a grazing permit The Forest Service argued in response that, under the CWA, only discharges from a point source or nonpoint source with a conveyance (i.e., a pipe or channel outlet) are regulated by the Act and, while cattle grazing may cause water pollution, it is not a regulated discharge under the Act. However, in its ruling, the court distinguished the definition of "discharge" from "discharge of a pollutant" from a point source and said that "pollution caused by cattle grazing constitutes a discharge into navigable waters within the meaning of section 401 of the Clean Water Act. Therefore, state certification under section 401 was required before the U.S. Forest Service issued a cattle grazing permit."

The ruling was seen by supporters as giving states new regulatory power over federal licenses or permits that affect water quality by clarifying that Section 401 applies to nonpoint source discharges of water pollution, in addition to point source discharges. Nonpoint source pollution includes rainfall and snowmelt runoff from farmlands, ranches, city streets, and similar areas. The ruling had the potential to give states a stronger hand in determining how federal lands should be managed. If so, the impact on states could be significant, since cattle grazing is a common activity on millions of acres of western lands managed by the Forest Service and the U.S. Bureau of Land Management, and states could face a substantial workload in processing Section 401 certifications for hundreds of grazing permits annually. Additional impacts could occur if Section 401 were held to apply to other types of federally permitted activities generally categorized as nonpoint sources, such as timber harvesting or logging.

Federal agencies disagreed over how to respond to the Oregon district court's ruling. EPA favored letting the decision stand, on the basis that nonpoint source pollution is the most significant contributor to water pollution in many states, and the decision would give states more power to manage it. The Agriculture Department (parent of the Forest Service), on the other hand, urged the Department of Justice to support an industry group's appeal of the case, and ultimately the government did join in appealing the decision.

In July 1998, a federal court of appeals reversed the district court's ruling, finding that cattle grazing on federal lands does not fall within the type of pollution covered by Section 401 of the Clean Water Act *(Oregon Natural Desert Association v. Dombeck,* 151 F.3d 945 (9th Cir., July 22, 1998)). The court maintained that Congress intended to permit direct federal regulation of effluent flowing from point sources, such as a pipe, ditch, or machine, but to regulate nonpoint source pollution only through federal grants, not through Section 401 water quality certification. In November 1999, the Supreme Court declined to review the case, thus leaving the matter as it was resolved by the court of appeals.

The State of Oregon had responded to the 1996 district court decision by adopting rules establishing a certification process for livestock grazing permits on federal lands in Oregon. However, after the court of appeals reversed that ruling and the Supreme Court declined to review it, the state withdrew the rules. Groups representing ranchers, farmers, and others were pleased that the district court's ruling was overturned, believing that Congress did not intend Section 401 to apply to nonpoint source pollution. Other CWA programs and tools such as financial incentives are better means of addressing nonpoint pollution problems, some say. Environmentalists disagree with the appeals court's conclusion and the legal outcome of the case, believing that Section 401 generally supports a broad reading that includes discharges from nonpoint sources.

In a broader context, some observers had viewed the district court's ruling as giving a boost to the ongoing process in a number of states to develop total maximum daily load (TMDL) allocations on pollution-impaired water bodies. Efforts to carry out this requirement in the Clean Water Act have been prompted recently by more than 40 lawsuits in 38 states against EPA and states, claiming they have failed to fulfill mandates in the law. In many cases, TMDLs are being developed to include nonpoint sources, as well as point sources, resulting in imposition of pollution control requirements and other measures to improve water quality and attain water quality standards. While the 9th Circuit's ruling did not directly affect the TMDL process, some persons believe that one result will be that nonpoint sources will be less involved in TMDL negotiations, leaving it mainly up to point sources to make the necessary water quality improvements.

So far, Congress has not responded to issues raised in the *Oregon Natural Desert* litigation. Nor was legislation introduced in the 105th or 106th Congress concerning licensing of hydroelectric facilities and the 1994 *PUD No. 1* case.

Legislative interest in Section 401 could increase in connection with recommendations on national energy policy by Vice President Cheney's National Energy Policy Development Group (NEPD Group).[3] It recommends that the hydroelectric licensing process administered by FERC undergo administrative and

---

[3] *National Energy Policy,* Report of the National Energy Policy Development Group, May 2001.

legislative reform so that hydropower can contribute to meeting the nation's energy needs. At the same time, a recent FERC report concludes that the most common cause of delayed hydropower licensing proceedings is untimely receipt of state water quality certification under the Clean Water Act.[4] Several legislative proposals in the 107th Congress (H.R. 1832, S. 71, and S. 388) would restrict the ability of the Departments of Interior and Commerce to impose conditions on hydropower projects concerning fishways at hydropower dams. The bills reflect concerns also discussed in the FERC report about delays caused by these and other federal agencies. Further, the Securing America's Future Energy (SAFE) Act of 2001, passed by the House in July, would allow FERC licensees to propose alternative fishway conditions, in lieu of conditions prescribed by Interior or Commerce (Division A, section 401 of H.R. 4). While these bills only address the roles of federal agencies hi hydropower licensing, not state certification under CWA Section 401, these water quality issues could be joined, as well, in the context of energy policy debate.

---

[4] Report to Congress prepared by the Staff of the Federal Energy Regulatory Commission. *Hydroelectric Licensing Policies, Procedures, and Regulations, Comprehensive Review and Recommendations.* May 2001. 145 p. See [http://www.ferc.gov/hydro/docs/section603.htm]

Chapter 3

CLEAN WATER ACTION PLAN:
BUDGETARY INITIATIVES

INTRODUCTION

In October 1997, Vice President Gore directed federal agencies to develop a Clean Water Initiative to improve and strengthen water pollution control efforts. The multi-agency initiative was released in February 1998. The President's FY1999 budget requested $2.5 billion ($609 million more than in FY1998) for five departments and agencies to fund this plan (the Clean Water Action Plan), which was considered primarily through the appropriations process. Congress passed bills to fund the Plan for FY1999, providing $2.0 billion, or less than 10% of the requested increases. In the FY2000 budget request, the Administration sought $450 million in increases ($2.5 billion total) for Plan activities. FY2000 appropriations bills provided $2.2 billion of the total requested. Congressional response to the Plan has reflected a mix of support for specific activities, along with some concern that the requests were taking funds away from other programs or projects having congressional priority. For FY2001, the budget requests $2.8 billion, a 27% increase above FY2000 levels.

In October 1997, on the 25th anniversary of the Clean Water Act, Vice President Al Gore announced an initiative intended to build on the environmental successes of the Act and to address the nation's remaining water quality challenges, especially nonpoint source pollution. The Vice President directed the Environmental Protection Agency (EPA) and the Department of Agriculture (USDA) to coordinate the work of other federal agencies to develop an action plan to improve and strengthen water pollution control efforts. The purpose of the plan is to achieve three goals: enhanced protection from public health threats posed by water pollution, more effective control of polluted runoff, and promotion of water quality protection on a watershed basis. Other departments involved include the Departments of Interior and Commerce, and the U.S. Army Corps of Engineers.

President Clinton and Vice President Gore released the action plan, called the Clean Water Action Plan (CWAP), in February 1998. Components of the plan, more than 100 actions, consist mainly of existing programs, including some planned regulatory actions that agencies have had underway, now to be enhanced with increased funding or accelerated with performance-specific deadlines. (Documents related to the CWAP are available at http://www.cleanwater.gov/.) The individual elements of the plan are built on four concepts: utilizing collaborative watershed-based partnerships to clean up impaired waters; maintaining strong federal and state standards; calling on federal natural resource and conservation agencies to assist in restoring and protecting watersheds; and ensuring that citizens and officials have improved information for decision making.

BUDGETARY SUPPORT FOR THE PLAN IN FY1999

The FY1999 budget identified the Clean Water Initiative as a high-priority for environmental programs in the budget. It requested a total of $2.47 billion -- a $609 million, or 33%, increase over 1998 base resources in relevant programs -- for multi-agency funding of a Clean Water and Watershed Restoration Initiative. It included funds for five departments and agencies, plus interagency funds. Almost one-half of the total FY1999 increases, $265 million, was designated as assistance to states and localities or individuals (farmers). Most of the activities were ongoing programs or projects. To a significant degree, including the additional resources in the FY1999 budget as a Clean Water and Watershed Restoration Initiative was more labeling or packaging of current activities than new undertakings, as the term "initiative" might typically imply.

By October 1998, Congress had passed three FY1999 appropriations bills (including an omnibus measure with funds for three of the departments) to fund the CWAP. The requests for increased funding met with mixed success. Over all, the enacted bills provided $2.0 billion, or 9.6% above FY1998 baseline amounts. The bills provided $179 million of the $609 million in requested increases. Two agencies received close to full funding for their requested action plan activities, but other agencies and departments received no or only small increases to support the plan.

The Administration sought $629 million for EPA's activities. This total was a $145 million increase above FY1998 baseline amounts, consisting of $95 million more for grants to states to manage nonpoint source pollution; $20 million more for grants for state administration of water quality programs; and $30 million for various EPA water quality activities, including development of water quality criteria for nutrients and updated regulations for animal feeding operations, and other grants for watershed restoration and wetlands protection. EPA received close to the full amount requested (in the VA-HUD, Independent Agencies Appropriations Bill, P.L. 105-276). Congress did approve the full $145 million increase, but this total was reduced by a 7% general reduction in one EPA account, with the result that it received $114 million more for state grants and $7 million more for EPA activities.

The Administration sought $903 million for USDA, $235 million above FY1998 funding. The largest increase, $100 million, was targeted to expand assistance to farmers under the Environmental Quality Incentives Program (EQIP) to $300 million annually. Established in the 1996 farm bill, EQIP provides farmers with assistance for structural or land management practices to protect water, soil, or related resources, with emphasis on problems of runoff from livestock production. USDA funds also included $110 million more for the Forest Service to address problems associated with abandoned mines, forest land management, and road maintenance. The Natural Resources Conservation Service (NRCS) was to receive $20 million for competitive grants to help communities build local capacity for watershed restoration work. The request included $2 million for the Agricultural Research Service for research on management practices to minimize loss of nutrients and pathogens from farm lands to the environment. Of the $235 million in requested increases for USDA, the appropriations bills provided $10 million more than FY1998 levels (in the Omnibus Consolidated and Supplemental Appropriations Act, P.L. 105-277). Notably, the Administration's request to increase funding for the EQIP program was not supported. P.L. 105-277 provided $26 million less for EQIP than in FY1998 ($176 million).

Several Department of Interior agencies were slated for increases totaling $59 million. Funds were included for the U.S. Geological Survey (U.S.G.S.) for monitoring and research to aid states with watershed assessment and work with other federal agencies concerning federal lands. Also included was additional funding for the Bureau of Land Management (BLM) for watershed health projects on western public lands; a 38% increase for the Office of Surface Mining's Clean Streams Initiative for cleanup of waters contaminated by runoff from abandoned coal mines; support for Fish and Wildlife Service partnership programs to protect and restore wetland ecosystems and habitats within critical watersheds (10% increase for the Partners for Fish and Wildlife Program and 26% increase for the North American Wetlands Conservation Fund); and funds for the Bureau of Indian Affairs to initiate water quality and watershed management planning for reservation lands in certain western river basins. The Department received $34 million of the requested increase (Department of the Interior and Related Agencies Appropriations Bill, in P.L. 105-277). This included small increases for U.S.G.S. water monitoring and assessment and for BLM work to improve water quality on federal lands.

The Administration requested $142 million for the Corps of Engineers, a $36 million increase above FY1998 funds. The bulk of the increase, $25 million, was intended to begin a new riverine ecosystem initiative, called Challenge 21, to plan and implement projects that restore watersheds while providing flood hazard mitigation for communities. It will use such non-traditional strategies as purchase of easements and land acquisition that have less impact on ecosystems than structural projects. Congress provided none of the additional funds sought for the Corps' activities under the CWAP (Energy and Water Development Appropriations Bill, P.L. 105-245), including rejecting funding for the proposed new Challenge 21 floodplain/riverine ecosystem restoration program. This initiative was considered separately by congressional authorizing committees, as part of proposals for water resources development legislation, but none was enacted by the 105th Congress.

Increases for the National Oceanic and Atmospheric Administration (NOAA), totaling $22 million, were to support grants to implement and develop Coastal Nonpoint Pollution Control programs ($12 million) and NOAA's participation in research, particularly concerning harmful algal blooms ($9 million). These increases were supported in large part (Departments of Commerce, Justice, State, the Judiciary and Related Agencies Appropriations Bill, in P.L. 105-277); Congress provided $17 million of the requested $22 million. However, both Appropriations Committees expressed concern about duplication between EPA and USDA programs.

Nearly 20% of the FY1999 budgetary initiative for the Clean Water Action Plan was intended to support two ongoing interagency projects, Florida Everglades restoration (funded mainly in the Department of the Interior Appropriations Bill, P.L. 105-277) and the California Bay-Delta program for ecosystem and water supply problems in California (funded in the Energy and Water Appropriations Bill, P.L.105-245). The President's budget had sought $112 million in increased funding for both projects (a 24% increase for the Everglades and a 68% increase for the Bay-Delta Program), adding to $308 million for

FY1998. Congress did not support increases for these projects and, in fact, provided level funding, compared with FY1998 levels. Still, the Bay-Delta program was singled out favorably in report language by both appropriations committees, despite the reduced funding.

FY2000 BUDGET REQUEST

In the FY2000 budget request, the Administration sought $2.49 billion total ($450 million in increases) for Clean Water Action Plan activities. In particular, the Administration renewed its requests to fund the EQIP program at $300 million and $25 million for the Corps of Engineers to establish the Challenge 21 program, as well as several sizeable increases above FY1999 levels: $25 million more for EPA program management activities; $75 million more for the Forest Service to improve water quality on federal lands; $25 million more for the Office of Surface Mining to address abandoned mine water quality problems; $81 million more ($312 million total) for multi-agency Florida Everglades restoration projects; and $20 million more ($95 million total) for the Bay-Delta program in California.

Appropriations to fund agencies' Plan activities were passed in four FY2000 bills (including an omnibus measure with funds for two of the departments). In total the bills provide $2.17 billion-$128 million more than in FY1999, but $322 million less than was requested. Appropriators again supported full funding for EPA's activities, but rejected a number of increases that the Administration sought: the EQIP program was again funded at $174 million, no funds were provided for Challenge 21 (although Congress authorized it in the Water Resources Development Act of 1999, P.L. 106-53), and funds for the Bay-Delta program totaled $60 million ($15 million less than in FY1999).

CONGRESSIONAL RESPONSE TO THE CWAP BUDGET

Congressional response to the budgetary initiatives to fund the Clean Water Action Plan has reflected a mix of support for the specific funding requests themselves, along with some concern that the budgetary requests were taking funds away from other programs or projects that have congressional priority. Administration documents accompanying the first budget requests in FY1999 indicated that financing for these activities would be deficit neutral and would be managed through transfers of funds available under discretionary spending caps and specific mandatory savings and revenue proposals elsewhere in the budget.

Nevertheless, the proposals did imply certain spending tradeoffs which raised concern with some interest groups and Members of Congress. For example, within the FY1999 proposal for EPA, the President requested a 17% increase for grants to states to support the Plan, but also requested 11% less for state revolving fund grants (to aid clean water and drinking water treatment construction) and 55% less for specially earmarked grants assisting water projects in needy cities. States and others urged Congress to support funding both for programs in the CWAP and other important environmental and water quality activities.

There is no single forum in Congress, either authorizing or appropriating committee, where the entire CWAP has been debated. On the budgetary side, where it has primarily been considered, the budget proposals are handled by five separate subcommittees of the Senate and House Appropriations Committees. Thus, there has been no single opportunity for comprehensive review or making funding tradeoffs where the several agencies are concerned, e.g., more for USDA, less for EPA.

Congress' actions providing less than full funding have not been extensively detailed in the Appropriations Committees' reports or in floor debates. Where explanations were noted, however, the principal reasons appeared to be budget constraints, as the Administration's requests competed with other priorities, including compliance with the 1997 balanced budget agreement,[1] and Congress not viewing some of the activities as new or significant enough to merit additional funding.[2] Further, it is not entirely clear why the Appropriations Committees were fully supportive of funding increases for EPA to implement the CWAP, but less so for the other departments and agencies. One possible explanation may be that subcommittee appropriators responsible for EPA are more familiar with water quality programs and, thus, may have viewed the budget request as a logical part of the agency's mission, compared with appropriators responsible for the other bills, for whom clean water activities could be viewed as less central. Appropriators responsible for EPA have historically supported the types of activities--especially grants for states--that are the bulk of the additional funds sought for that agency.

---

[1] For example, the House Appropriations Committee noted, concerning a Forest Service request to fund rangeland management activities, "The Committee does not have the resources to fund any of the $16,000,000 increase requested as part of the President's clean water initiative." U.S. House. Committee on Appropriations. Department of the Interior and Related Agencies Appropriations Bill, 1999, Report to accompany H.R. 4193. (H.Rept. 105-609) p. 77.

[2] Likewise, the House Committee said, concerning a request for funds for the U.S. Geological Survey, "The Committee has not provided any funds for the Administration's so called clean water initiative, which from the Committee's perspective is mostly a repackaging of existing programs that have been funded and supported by the Congress." Ibid., p. 49.

In several Statements of Administration Policy presented during the appropriations process, the Office of Management and Budget has expressed concern about elements of the CWAP left unfunded or underfunded. Stakeholder groups also have urged Congress to provide full funding, if the Plan's objectives are to be met. However, the budgetary elements were split among several groups of appropriators, making it more difficult for supporters to make the case for funding the Plan as a whole.

EPA and USDA officials hold the view that the Plan will be implemented, even though appropriations have been less than requested. Implementation will occur, they say, because they believe that the Plan's many actions are the only way to achieve the Clean Water Act's water quality goals, especially for management of nonpoint sources of pollution. A lack of new resources will mean a 50- or 100-year implementation schedule for states, the federal government, and other participants, rather than the 25 years believed to be needed to complete the agenda as it was presented in February 1998.

FY2001 BUDGET REQUEST

For FY2001, the President's budget requests $2.76 billion for activities under the Clean Water Action Plan, a 27% increase ($584 million) above the FY2000 enacted funding level of $2.2 billion. Several agencies' programs would receive increases under this budget. The Administration seeks $159 million in additional funding for EPA, consisting of $50 million for state grants to manage nonpoint (runoff) pollution problems, $45 million for state grants for general administration of water quality programs, $50 million for a new state grant program to assist with cleanup of Great Lakes contamination problems, and $14 million for EPA activities.

The Administration seeks $151 million in additional funding for USDA's EQIP program (for a total of $325 million), again renewing a request to expand this conservation assistance program. Other proposed increases for USDA include $54 million more for technical assistance concerning animal waste management (appropriators provided $19 million for this activity for FY2000) and $85 million more for Forest Service activities to improve water quality on federal lands (appropriators provided $542 million for this activity for FY2000, $36 million less than had been requested).

Among the other increases included in the President's budget are: $15 million more for wetlands restoration in the budget of the Fish and Wildlife Service (for a total of $58 million); $7 million more for NOAA's coastal pollution and research programs (for a total of $22 million, as requested for each of the last 2 years); $8 million more for the Corps of Engineers' wetlands regulatory program (for a total of $125 million) and $20 million for the Corps' newly-authorized Challenge 21 program; and $50 million more for the multi-agency Florida Everglades restoration program (for a total of $334 million).

Chapter 4

WATER QUALITY: IMPLEMENTING THE CLEAN WATER ACT

INTRODUCTION

Congress enacted the most recent major amendments to the Clean Water Act in 1987 (P.L. 100-4). Since then, the Environmental Protection Agency (EPA), states, and others have been working to implement the many program changes and additions mandated in the law. At issue today–30 years after enactment of the core law–is what progress is being made to achieve its goals. In general, states and environmental groups fault EPA for delays in issuing guidance and assistance needed to carry out the provisions of the law. EPA and others are critical of states, in turn, for not reaching beyond conventional knowledge and approaches to address their water quality problems. Environmental groups have been criticized for insufficient recognition of EPA's and states' need for flexibility to implement the Act. Finally, Congress has been criticized for not providing adequate resources to meet EPA and state needs.

Three issues have predominated recently in connection with implementation of the law. The first involves requirements under current law for states to develop total maximum daily loads (TMDLs) to restore pollution-impaired waters. The second issue involves the nonpoint pollution management provisions added in 1987. States are developing management programs describing methods that will be used to reduce nonpoint pollution, which may be responsible for as much as 50% of the nation's remaining water quality problems. Most observers agree that implementation of nonpoint source control measures is significantly hindered by lack of resources, including federal assistance. EPA adopted program guidance intended to give states more flexibility and to speed up progress in nonpoint source control.

The third issue is funding to construct municipal wastewater treatment plants under the State Revolving Fund provisions of the 1987 amendments. Budgetary constraints on federal aid for wastewater treatment and large remaining funding needs are a continuing concern.

Reauthorization of the Act was on the agenda of the 104th Congress, when the House passed H.R. 961, but no amendments were enacted. No major legislative activity occurred in the 105th or 106th Congresses, although legislation was passed affecting some individual program areas. In the 107th Congress, legislation focused on water infrastructure funding legislation, but no bill was enacted. Recent attention also has focused on EPA rules for the Act's TMDL program issued in 2000.

The Bush Administration has proposed few new clean water initiatives. However, on January 13, the Agency announced a Water Quality Trading Policy intended as an innovative approach to assist industry and municipalities in meeting Clean Water Act obligations.

MOST RECENT DEVELOPMENTS

On February 20, 5 months after the start of the fiscal year, President Bush signed legislation providing FY2003 appropriations for EPA and other non-defense agencies (P.L. 108-7). The act provides $1.34 billion in grant funds for state clean water infrastructure (SRF) programs, plus $405 million in special project grants earmarked by the legislation. The President presented his FY2004 budget request on February 3, requesting $850 million for clean water SRF grants.

On December 15, 2002, the EPA Administrator signed final revised rules to regulate waste discharges from large animal feedlots (termed confined animal feeding operations, CAFOs). EPA estimates that 15,500 CAFOs will need to obtain clean water permits to comply with the rules, compared with 26,000-39,000 that would have been regulated under the Clinton Administration's proposed rule. Environmental advocates criticized the final rules for inadequately addressing animal waste runoff problems, while farm groups said the rules generally are workable.

The Bush Administration is continuing its review of controversial regulations issued by the Clinton Administration in 2000 to strengthen existing rules that govern a Clean Water Act (CWA) program intended to restore impaired waters, the Total Maximum Daily Load (TMDL) program. On December 20, 2002, EPA proposed to withdraw the 2000 TMDL rule while it considers initiating an entirely new rule or other options; no further timeframe was announced.

BACKGROUND AND ANALYSIS
THE ACT AND RECENT AMENDMENTS

The Federal Water Pollution Control Act, or Clean Water Act, is the principal law concerned with polluting activity in the nation's streams, lakes, and estuaries. Originally enacted in 1948, it was totally revised by amendments in 1972 (P.L. 92-500) that gave the Act its current form and spelled out ambitious programs for water quality improvements that are now being put in place by industries and cities. Congress made certain fine-tuning amendments in 1977 (P.L. 95-217) and 1981 (P.L. 97-117) and enacted the most recent major amendments in 1987 (P.L. 100-4).

The Act consists of two major parts: regulatory provisions that impose progressively more stringent requirements on industries and cities in order to meet the statutory goal of zero discharge of pollutants, and provisions that authorize federal financial assistance for municipal wastewater treatment construction. Industries were to meet pollution control limits first by use of Best Practicable Technology and later by improved Best Available Technology. Cities were to achieve secondary treatment of municipal wastewater (roughly 85% removal of conventional wastes), or better if needed to meet water quality standards. Both major parts are supported by research activities authorized in the law, plus permit and penalty provisions for enforcement. Programs are administered by the Environmental Protection Agency (EPA), while state and local governments have the principal day-to-day responsibility for implementing the law.

The most recent major amendments to the law are the Water Quality Act of 1987 (P.L. 100-4). These amendments culminated 6 years of congressional efforts to extend and revise the Act and are the most comprehensive amendments to it since 1972. They recognize that, despite much progress to date, significant water quality problems persist. Among its many provisions, the 1987 legislation:

- established a comprehensive program for controlling toxic pollutant discharges, beyond that already provided in the Act, to respond to so-called "toxic hot spots;"

- added a program requiring states to develop and implement programs to control nonpoint sources of pollution, or rainfall runoff from farm and urban areas, plus construction, forestry, and mining sites;

- authorized a total of $18 billion for wastewater treatment assistance under a combination of the Act's traditional construction grants program through FY1990 and, as a transition to full state funding responsibility, a new program of grants to capitalize State Revolving Funds, from FY1989-1994;

- authorized or modified a number of programs to address water pollution problems in diverse geographic areas such as coastal estuaries, the Great Lakes, and the Chesapeake Bay; and

- revised many of the Act's regulatory, permit, and enforcement programs.

Legislative activity after P.L. 100-4

Congressional oversight of water quality issues was limited following enactment of P.L. 100-4. Subcommittees held general oversight hearings, as well as several hearings on individual issues (wetlands protection, Chesapeake Bay programs, and toxics contamination of Great Lakes waters), but reserved extensive review and oversight until implementation had been underway for some time.

EPA, states, industry, and other citizens continue to implement the 1987 legislation, including meeting the numerous requirements and deadlines in it. Three sets of issues have been the focus of attention regarding the pace and effectiveness of implementation: the toxic pollutant control provisions, nonpoint pollution management provisions, and the State Revolving Fund provisions to transfer wastewater treatment funding responsibility to the states after 1994. Attention has also focused on the cost-effectiveness of clean water requirements and flexibility of implementation.

Implementation issues discussed below were the basis for legislation to reauthorize the Clean Water Act during the 103rd Congress. Committees held hearings in 1993, and the Senate Environment and Public Works Committee reported a comprehensive reauthorization bill, S. 2093, in May 1994. Legislation also was introduced in the House, but no further action occurred because of controversies specific to the Act and the pending bills, as well as controversies over regulatory relief issues that became barriers to a number of bills in 1994.

In the 104th Congress, the House moved quickly on Clean Water Act legislation, approving a comprehensive reauthorization bill in May 1995. H.R. 961 would have amended many of the regulatory and standards provisions of the law, required EPA to use extensive new risk assessment and cost-benefit analysis procedures, and increased flexibility with regulatory relief from current clean water programs. However, the Senate did not take up the Clean Water Act during the 104th Congress; thus, no legislation was enacted.

1997 marked the 25-year anniversary of the 1972 Clean Water Act amendments, which established the goals, objectives, and structure that continue to guide the law today. In the 105th Congress, no major committee activity over the Act occurred either in the House or the Senate. In the 106th Congress, legislative attention focused on individual program areas of the law; no comprehensive reauthorization legislation was introduced. However, activity on bills dealing with specific water quality issues did occur. Congress passed a bill to strengthen protection of coastal recreation waters through upgraded water quality standards and coastal waters monitoring programs (P.L. 106-284). Congress also passed a bill reauthorizing several existing CWA programs (i.e., Chesapeake Bay, clean lakes, and the National Estuary Program; P.L. 106-457). Further, Congress passed a bill to authorize CWA grant funding for wet weather sewerage projects (included as a provision of P.L. 106-554, FY2001 Consolidated Appropriations bill). In the 107th Congress, attention was focused on bills to authorize funding for water infrastructure projects, but no legislation was enacted. However, before adjournment, Congress approved the Great Lakes Legacy Act (P.L. 107-303), which authorizes $200 million for EPA to carry out projects to remediate sediment contamination in the Great Lakes.

More generally, following the September 11, 2001 terrorist attacks on the World Trade Center and the Pentagon, congressional attention has focused on security, preparedness, and emergency response issues. Among the many topics of interest is protection of the nation's water infrastructure facilities (both wastewater and drinking water) from possible physical damage, biological/chemical attacks, and cyber disruption. Policymakers are considering a number of legislative options in this area, including enhanced physical security, communication and coordination, and research. Physical security of wastewater treatment plant operations is one of the issues under consideration. In October 2002, the House passed legislation to provide $200 million in grants for security activities at wastewater treatment plants (H.R. 5169). Similar legislation was introduced in the Senate (S. 3037), but no further action occurred. In the 108th Congress, H.R. 866 was introduced on February 13 and approved by the House

Transportation and Infrastructure Committee on February 26; it is identical to H.R. 5169 as passed in the 107th Congress.

Although much progress has been made in achieving the ambitious goals established in the law 30 years ago to restore the maintain the chemical, physical, and biological integrity of rivers, lakes, and coastal waters, problems persist. Based on the limited water quality monitoring that is done by states, EPA recently reported in the 2000 National Water Quality Inventory Report that 39% of assessed river and stream miles and 45% of assessed lake acres do not meet applicable water quality standards and were found to be impaired for one or more desired uses. The types of remaining water quality problems are diverse, ranging from runoff from farms and ranches, city streets, and other diffuse sources to metals (especially mercury), organic and inorganic toxic substances discharged from factories and sewage treatment plants, as well as nonpoint sources.

The Bush Administration has been reviewing a number of current clean water programs and rules but has proposed few new initiatives. However, on January 13, the Agency announced a Water Quality Trading Policy intended as an innovative approach to assist industry and municipalities in meeting Clean Water Act obligations. Trading allows one source to meet regulatory requirements by using pollutant reductions created by another source that has lower pollution control costs. The policy revises a May 2002 proposal which reflected lessons learned from a similar policy issued by the Clinton Administration in 1996. Water quality or effluent trading projects have occurred in the United States since the early 1980s.

TOTAL MAXIMUM DAILY LOAD (TMDL) REQUIREMENTS

Section 303(d) of the Clean Water Act requires states to identify pollutant-impaired water segments and develop "total maximum daily loads" (TMDLs) that set the maximum amount of pollution that a water body can receive without violating water quality standards. If a state fails to do so, EPA is required to develop a priority list for the state and make its own TMDL determination. Most states have lacked the resources to do TMDL analyses, which involve complex assessment of point and nonpoint sources and mathematical modeling, and EPA has both been reluctant to override states and has also lacked resources to do the analyses. Thus, for many years there was little implementation of the provision that Congress enacted in 1972. In recent years, national and local environmental groups have filed more than 40 lawsuits in 38 states against EPA and states for failure to fulfill requirements of the Act. Of the suits tried or settled to date, 19 have resulted in court orders requiring expeditious development of TMDLs. EPA and state officials have been concerned about diverting resources from other high-priority water quality activities in order to meet the courts' orders. In 1996, EPA created an advisory committee to solicit advice on the TMDL problem. Recommendations from the advisory committee formed the basis of program changes that EPA proposed in August 1999. The 1999 proposal set forth criteria for states, territories, and authorized Indian tribes to identify impaired waters and establish all TMDLs within 15 years. It would require more comprehensive assessments of waterways, detailed cleanup plans, and timetables for implementation.

The 1999 proposal was highly controversial because of issues such as burdens on states to implement a revised TMDL program and potential impacts on some agriculture and forestry sources which are not now subject to CWA regulations. The controversies also have drawn congressional attention, and 13 congressional hearings were held during the 106th Congress by four separate House and Senate committees. Public and congressional pressure on EPA to revise or withdraw the TMDL proposal entirely was great. Several legislative proposals to modify EPA's TMDL proposals or delay implementation of final rules were introduced

TMDL issues also were addressed in FY2001 appropriations bills. Before the July 4, 2000, congressional recess, the House and Senate approved a FY2001 Military Construction and emergency supplemental appropriations bill (H.R. 4425, H.Rept. 106-710) that included a provision to prevent EPA from spending any funds in FY2000 or FY 2001 to finalize or implement new TMDL rules. President Clinton signed the bill on July 13, 2000, in spite of the TMDL restriction, which the Administration opposed (P.L. 106-246). However, the EPA Administrator signed the new rules on July 11 but delayed the effective date until October 2001 when the limitation in P.L. 106-246 would expire. EPA's signing of the rule before the rider took effect led to more criticism.

The FY2001 appropriations act providing funds for EPA, P.L. 106-377, included report language mandating studies by the National Academy of Sciences (NAS) and EPA on the scientific basis of the TMDL program and on the potential costs to states and businesses of implementing the revised TMDL rules. The NAS report, examining the role of science in the TMDL program, was issued June 15, 2001. It did not specifically analyze the July 2000 revised regulations. The NAS panel concluded that scientific knowledge exists to move forward with the TMDL program and recommended that EPA and states use adaptive implementation for TMDL development. In many cases, the report said, water quality problems and solutions are obvious and should proceed without complex analysis. In other cases, solutions are more complex and require a different level of understanding and something like phased implementation. A House Transportation Committee subcommittee held a hearing on the NAS report on June 28, 2001. In August 2001, EPA issued a draft report on costs of the 2000 TMDL program. It estimates that average annual costs to states and EPA of developing TMDLs could be $63-$69 million, while implementation costs for pollutant sources could be between $900 million and $4.3 billion per year, depending on states' actions. The General Accounting Office recently reported that inconsistent monitoring, data collection, and listing procedures used by states to identify impaired waters have hindered efforts to develop effective TMDL programs (*Water Quality: Inconsistent State Approaches Complicate Nation's Efforts to Identify Its Most Polluted Waters*, GAO-02-186).

The Bush Administration announced in October 2001 that it would delay the effective date of the 2000 rule until April 30, 2003, to allow for further review. That announcement came after a federal court granted the Administration's request for a similar 18-month suspension of litigation which is challenging the regulation (nearly a dozen interest groups sued EPA over various parts of the TMDL rule). In the interim, current program requirements under existing regulations and court-sanctioned TMDL schedules remain in place. A House Transportation and Infrastructure subcommittee held an oversight hearing in November 2001 concerning EPA's plans to revise the rule. Most recently, on December 22, 2002, EPA proposed to withdraw the July 2000 TMDL rule while it considers initiating an entirely new rule or other options; no further timeframe was announced. EPA officials said that additional time beyond May 2003 is needed to decide whether and how to revise the current program and that allowing the rule to take effect on April 30 would be disruptive of ongoing review efforts.

NONPOINT POLLUTION MANAGEMENT

The 1987 amendments added a new Section 319 to the Act, under which states were required to develop and implement programs to control nonpoint sources of pollution, or rainfall runoff from farm and urban areas, as well as construction, forestry, and mining sites. Previously, the Act had largely focused on controlling point sources, while helping states and localities to plan for management of diverse nonpoint sources. Yet, as industrial and municipal sources have abated pollution, uncontrolled nonpoint sources have become a relatively larger portion of remaining water quality problems—perhaps contributing as much as 50% of the nation's water pollution.

States were required to identify waters not expected to meet water quality standards— because of nonpoint source pollution and to implement plans for managing pollution from runoff. Federal grants totaling $400 million were authorized to cover as much as 60% of the costs of implementing a state's management plan.

The funding issue has become more urgent as states have moved from assessment and plan development to management, since Congress intended that Section 319 funds be used primarily to implement nonpoint pollution controls on the ground. EPA has urged states to use a portion of monies that they receive under Section 106 of the Act, water quality program assistance grants, for nonpoint source activities. But, doing so utilizes money otherwise needed for core state efforts, such as permit issuance, monitoring, enforcement, etc. Several concerns have been raised about the Section 319 program.

Adequacy of Plans

Whether state plans have comprehensively addressed nonpoint pollution problems is a lingering question. Some environmental groups criticize EPA for providing inadequate guidance on methods, or management practices, to advance control of nonpoint sources beyond known problems and existing implementation steps, such as voluntary compliance and public education. Moreover, some believe that states should be required to repeat the nonpoint source assessments, which were one-time-only activities under the 1987 law, in order to reflect improvements in technical and scientific information.

Quality of Plans

EPA officials acknowledge that the quality of assessment reports and management plans was quite variable and that many (including some that have been approved) were disappointing. Several reasons were cited: staff limitations affecting states' and EPA regions' ability to prepare and oversee plans; lack of funding; limited federal clout, since the program is essentially voluntary; and variations in the way regions administered the program.

Funding

Precise estimates of the cost to manage nonpoint source pollution are not available, but in 1994 EPA estimated that current and planned spending by private sources, states, and cities under provisions of current law is between $750 million and $1.1 billion per year. Without adequate funding to implement state management plans, it is doubtful that much will be achieved under Section 319 to control nonpoint source pollution. Lack of funding risks the possibility of Section 319 becoming the Section 208 of this decade: in the 1970s, states and regions prepared areawide waste treatment management plans under Section 208 of this Act, intended to comprehensively cover point and nonpoint sources. No implementation monies were authorized, and few of the plans were realized, as a result.

Program Changes

EPA and states negotiated changes intended to give the 319 program a new framework by giving states more flexibility. As a result, in 1996, EPA issued revised guidance concerning state management of nonpoint source programs that is intended to recognize that federal and state processes need to be streamlined to increase program effectiveness and to speed progress towards solving nonpoint pollution problems. The revised guidance outlines nine key elements to be reflected in state programs (e.g., strong partnerships with stakeholders, explicit short and long term goals for protecting surface and ground waters). States that meet the nine criteria can be designated as leadership states, making them eligible for incentives such as multi-year grants, reduced amount and frequency of reporting, and self-assessment by states themselves. These incentives contrast with the previous program approach, in which states competed for grants and those which did not meet particular requirements received less grant money.

Significance for TMDLs

Attention has focused on nonpoint source management efforts as a result of recent emphasis by EPA and states on meeting TMDL requirements (see **TMDL** discussion, above). Scrutiny of nonpoint pollution problems and how they are being addressed has intensified as policymakers and program officials assess additional steps to continue progress towards the Act's water quality goals. EPA has recently begun to explicitly link implementation of Section 319 with TMDL activities. For example, in September 2001, EPA published guidance saying that grants awarded under Section 319 should have a concentrated focus on the development and implementation of TMDLs for nonpoint sources of pollution, although funds will still be awarded to activities other than TMDLs. However, states and agricultural interests criticized the guidance as being too restrictive, and in August 2002, EPA modified the guidance which continues to encourage development of nonpoint source TMDLs but gives states more flexibility to do so, especially in areas that lack formally-established TMDLs.

STATE REVOLVING FUND PROGRAM

The Act's program of financial aid for municipal wastewater treatment plant construction was a central and controversial aspect of debate on the 1987 amendments. Since 1972 Congress has provided $73 billion to assist wastewater treatment construction, but funding needs remain very high: an additional $139.5 billion nationwide over the next 20 years for all types of projects eligible for funding under the Act, according to the most recent estimate by EPA and the states completed in 1996. On September 30, EPA released a study, called the Gap Analysis, which assesses the difference between current spending for wastewater infrastructure and total funding needs (both capital and operation and maintenance). EPA estimates that, over the next two decades, the United States needs to spend nearly $390 billion to replace existing wastewater infrastructure systems and to build new ones. Funding needs for operation and maintenance are an additional $148 billion, the Agency estimates. According to the study, if there is no increase in investment, there will be about a $6 billion gap between current annual capital expenditures for wastewater treatment ($13 billion annually) and projected spending needs. The study also estimates that, if wastewater spending increases by 3% annually, the gap would shrink by nearly 90% (to about $1 billion annually). At issue has been what should be the federal role in assisting states and cities, especially in view of such high projected funding needs.

The 1987 amendments extended through FY1990 the traditional Title II program of grants for sewage treatment project construction, under which the federal share was 55% of project costs. The 1987 law initiated a program of grants to capitalize State Water Pollution Control Revolving Funds (SRFs), or loan programs, in a new Title VI. States are required to deposit an amount equal to at least 20% of the federal capitalization grant in the Fund established under Title VI. Under the revolving fund concept, monies used for wastewater treatment construction would be repaid by loan recipients to the states (repayment was not required for grants under the Title II program), to be recycled for future construction in other communities, thus providing an ongoing source of financing. The expectation in 1987 was that the federal contributions to SRFs would assist in making a transition to full state and local financing by FY1995. Although most states believe that the SRF is working well, early funding and administrative problems have delayed the anticipated shift to full state responsibility. Thus, SRF issues have been prominent on the Clean Water Act reauthorization agenda in recent Congresses.

SRF monies may be used for certain types of financial activity, including loans for as much as 100% of project costs (at or below market interest rates, including interest-free loans), to buy or refinance cities' debt obligation, or as a source of revenue or security for payment of principal and interest on a state-issued bond. SRF monies also may be used to provide loan guarantees or credit enhancement for localities.

Loans made by a state from its SRF are to be used first to assure progress towards the goals of the Act and, in particular, on projects to meet the standards and enforceable requirements of the Act. After states achieve those requirements of the Act, SRF monies also may be used to implement nonpoint pollution management and national estuary programs.

Table 1 summarizes wastewater treatment funding under Title II (traditional grants program) and Title VI (capitalization grants for revolving loan programs). (**Note: Table 1** does *not* include appropriations for special project grants in individual cities.)

One issue of interest is impacts on small communities. These entities in particular have found it difficult to participate in the SRF loan program, since many are characterized by narrow or weak tax bases, limited or no access to capital markets, lower relative household incomes, and higher per capita needs. They often find it harder to borrow to meet their capital needs and pay relatively high premiums to do so. Meeting the special needs of small towns, through a reestablished grant program, other funding source, or loan program with special rules, has been an issue of interest to Congress.

Congressional oversight of wastewater/SRF issues has focused on several points, including: many small communities have found it difficult to participate in the SRF loan program, and the lack of funds for high-cost categories of projects such as correcting combined sewer overflows. Although there has been some criticism of the SRF program, and debate continues over specific concerns (such as small community impacts), the basic approach is well supported in Congress and elsewhere. Congress used the clean water SRF as the model when it established a drinking water SRF in the Safe Drinking Water Act in 1996 (P.L. 104-182).

Table 1. Wastewater Treatment Funding
(billions of dollars)

Fiscal Year	Authorizations		Appropriations	
	Title II	Title VI	Title II	Title VI
1986	$2.4	—	$1.8	—
1987	2.4	—	2.36	—
1988	2.4	—	2.3	—
1989	1.2	1.2	0.941	0.941
1990	1.2	1.2	0.967	0.967
1991	—	2.4	—	2.1
1992	—	1.8	—	1.95
1993	—	1.2	—	1.93
1994	—	0.6	—	1.22
1995	—	—	—	1.24
1996	—	—	—	2.07
1997	—	—	—	0.625
1998	—	—	—	1.35
1999	—	—	—	1.35
2000	—	—	—	1.345
2001	—	—	—	1.35
2002	—	—	—	1.35
2003	—	—	—	1.34

OTHER ISSUES

A number of other Clean Water Act issues continue to receive attention, as well. Like those discussed previously, many of these topics have recently been part of Congress' agenda in connection with reauthorization.

Stormwater Discharges

EPA has struggled since the 1970s to regulate industrial and municipal stormwater discharges in a workable yet comprehensive manner. In P.L. 100- 4 Congress established firm deadlines and priorities for EPA to require permits for these discharges of stormwater that is not mixed or contaminated with household or industrial waste. EPA issued rules in November 1990 (21 months after the statutory deadline) that addressed the process of applying for stormwater permits. The Agency worked with an advisory committee of stakeholders beginning in 1994 to develop rules for regulating smaller stormwater dischargers, which were not covered by EPA's 1990 rules. Rules for smaller dischargers (unregulated industries and small cities) were issued in October 1999. The burden of complying with the rules continues to be an issue with many affected industries and municipalities, especially small cities, which face compliance deadlines in March 2003.

Combined and Separate Sewer Overflows

A total of 772 municipalities have combined sewers where domestic sanitary sewage, industrial wastes, infiltration from groundwater, and stormwater runoff are collected. These systems serve approximately 40 million persons, mainly in older urban and coastal cities. Normally (under dry-weather conditions), the combined wastes are conveyed to a municipal sewage treatment plant.

Properly designed, sized, and maintained combined sewers can be an acceptable part of a city's water pollution control infrastructure. However, combined sewer overflow (CSO) occurs when the capacity of the collection and treatment system is exceeded due to high volumes of rainwater or snowmelt, and the excess volume is diverted and discharged directly into receiving waters, bypassing the sewage treatment plants. Often the excess flow that contains raw sewage, industrial wastes, and stormwater is discharged untreated. Many combined sewer systems are found in coastal areas where recreational areas, fish habitat and shellfish beds may be contaminated by the discharges.

In 1994 EPA issued a CSO permitting strategy after negotiations with key stakeholder groups. Cities were to implement nine minimum controls by January 1, 1997 (e.g., proper operation and maintenance programs for sewer systems and pollution prevention programs). The EPA strategy did not contain a deadline for issuance of permits or for controlling CSOs. Deadlines will be contained in plans developed by permitting authorities, which primarily are states. Controls are available and generally are based on combinations of management techniques (such as temporary retention of excess flow during storm events) and structural measures (ranging from screens that capture solids to construction of separate sewer systems). EPA officials stated in 1998 that only about one-half of the cities with combined sewers implemented the minimum measures called for in the 1994 strategy. EPA is now working with states to remind cities of their obligations to address CSO problems. However, a formal enforcement strategy is not contemplated.

A more recent issue concerning some cities is the problem of overflows from municipal separate sanitary sewers (SSOs) that are not CSOs because they transport only sanitary wastes. Discharges of untreated sewage from these sewers occur from manholes, broken pipes and deteriorated infrastructure, and undersized pipes, and can occur in wet or dry weather. EPA estimates that there are about 18,000 municipalities with separate sanitary sewers, all of which can, under certain circumstances, experience overflows. No explicit EPA or statutory control policy currently exists. In 1995, EPA convened a stakeholders' group to discuss how to address those overflows that pose the highest environmental and public health risk first. On January 5, 2001, the Clinton Administration finalized regulations to improve the operation of municipal sanitary sewer collection systems, reduce the frequency and occurrence of overflows, clarify the existing CWA prohibition on SSO discharges, and clarify circumstances appropriate for enforcement action. The new rules, not yet published, are being reviewed by the Bush Administration.

Funding CSO and SSO projects is a major concern of states and cities. In December 2000, the 106th Congress passed legislation, the Wet Weather Water Quality Act, authorizing a 2-year $1.5 billion grants program to reduce wet weather flows from municipal sewer systems. This bill was included in H.R. 4577, the FY2001 Consolidated Appropriations bill (Section 112 of Division B, P.L. 106-554). The measure also codified EPA's 1994 CSO policy on sewer overflows (discussed above).

Wetlands

Public debate over the nation's wetlands has come to focus on questions of the effectiveness and costs of wetland resource protection efforts, rather than on whether such resources should be preserved. The permit program authorized by Section 404 of the Clean Water Act is one of the major federal programs that protects wetlands. However, environmentalists and others have criticized Section 404 as being inadequate to prevent the continuing loss of wetlands, due to statutory exemption of certain types of actions on farmlands and weak enforcement. Those wishing to develop wetlands maintain that existing laws are already an intrusion on private land-use decisions and that further federal involvement is unwarranted. How best to protect remaining wetlands and regulate activities taking place in wetlands has become one of the most contentious environmental policy issues facing Congress and was a prominent element of clean water debate during the 103rd and 104th Congresses. The 107th Congress examined few wetlands issues, and the main activity concerned wetlands provisions of omnibus farm bill legislation. Although there was no legislative activity on Section 404, committee hearings were held on several issues arising from judicial decisions, administrative actions of interest, and implementation of current law. For example, in October 2001, the House Transportation and Infrastructure Water Resources and Environment Subcommittee held an oversight hearing on enforcement of wetlands regulatory programs, hearing from a number of witnesses who claimed to have been treated improperly by federal regulators and enforcement officials. In September 2002, the House Government Reform Subcommittee on Energy Policy, Natural Resources and Regulatory Affairs held a hearing on the government's response to a 2001 Supreme Court case which narrowed the government's regulatory jurisdiction over isolated waters, *Solid Waste Agency of Northern Cook County (SWANCC) v. U.S. Army Corps of Engineers* (531 U.S. 159 (2001)). Committee Members and public witnesses indicated that a lack of guidance on the government's interpretation of the case has led to inconsistent regulatory decisions in individual regions of the country.

Strategy Concerning Animal Feeding Operations

Public and policy attention has been increasing on steps to minimize public health and environmental impacts of runoff from animal feeding operations (AFOs). AFOs are agricultural facilities that confine livestock feeding activities, thus concentrating animal populations and waste. Animal waste is frequently applied to land for disposal and to utilize the nutrient value of manure to benefit crops. If not managed properly, however, it can pose risks to water quality and public health, contributing pollutants such as nutrients, sediment, pathogens, and ammonia to the environment. In 1999, EPA and the U.S. Department of Agriculture initiated a national AFO strategy to improve compliance and strengthen existing regulations that are intended to control adverse environmental impacts of these agricultural activities.

Existing EPA regulations, issued in the 1970s, require CWA discharge permits for the largest AFOs, termed confined animal feeding operations (CAFOs). However, EPA acknowledges that compliance and enforcement of these permit rules has been poor (less than one-third of covered facilities actually have permits) and that the regulations themselves are outdated. For example, they do not reflect changed waste management practices or address the need for management plans dealing with land application of manure. The 1999 national strategy contains a number of short-term and long-term steps to improve compliance and strengthen existing regulations, obtain better information through data collection and research on water quality impairments due to AFOs, and together with other federal agencies and states, coordinate activities related to AFOs. In December 2000, EPA proposed rules to increase the number of AFOs required to obtain CWA permits and to restrict land application of animal wastes. In May 2001, a House Transportation and Infrastructure subcommittee held an oversight hearing on the December regulatory proposal. Issues that Congress has addressed during this period include impacts and costs imposed on the agricultural sector, especially small farmers, and how the proposed combination of regulatory and incentivebased measures in the 1999 National AFO Strategy will achieve control of agricultural runoff that adversely affects water quality. In legislation providing FY2000 funding for EPA (P.L. 106-74), Congress directed EPA in conjunction with USDA to submit a report to Congress by May 15, 2001, providing a cost and capability assessment of the AFO strategy. This report was expected to be delivered to Congress in December 2001.

On December 15, 2002, the EPA Administrator signed final revised rules to regulate waste discharges from CAFOs. The final rules, which the Agency was under court order to issue by December 2002, modified the Clinton Administration's 2000 proposal in a number of areas. The final rules retain much of the structure of the existing rules, such as regulatory thresholds and definitions, but include requirements for development of nutrient management plans to better manage land application of manure. EPA estimates that 15,500 CAFOs will be regulated by these rules (compared with 26,000-39,000 under the proposal), at an annual compliance cost of $335 million (versus $850 million-$980 million under the proposal). The final rules dropped a controversial proposal to require co-permitting of integrators (large companies that contract with farmers to raise livestock), as well as the farmers themselves. Farm groups said that the regulations are generally workable and consistent with environmental initiatives in the 2002 farm bill (P.L. 107-171), but environmental groups are criticizing the rules for inadequately addressing animal waste runoff problems. A January 2003 GAO report concludes that the new rules will be ineffective unless EPA increases its oversight of state regulatory programs, which have primary responsibility for ensuring compliance by feedlot operators (*Increased EPA Oversight Will Improve Environmental Program for Concentrated Animal Feeding Operations*, GAO-03-285.)

CONTINUING ISSUE:
APPROPRIATIONS AND THE FEDERAL BUDGET

Although the 1987 Clean Water Act amendments dealt extensively with financial aid issues, funding questions have continued to arise and be addressed in the context of appropriations.

FY2003

The Bush Administration presented its FY2003 budget request on February 4, 2002. It sought a total $1.335 billion for clean water infrastructure funds (compared with $1.8 billion appropriated for FY2002), consisting of $1.212 billion for clean water SRF grants and $123 million for a limited number of special projects (especially in Alaska Native Villages and in communities on the U.S.-Mexico border). The Administration eliminated funds for unrequested project spending that Congress earmarked in the FY2002 law which totaled $344 million. Also, the Administration requested no funds for the municipal sewer overflow grants program authorized in 2000 in P.L. 106-554 (discussed above). The FY2003 budget included a request to establish a $20 million grant program for a Targeted Watersheds Project in a limited number of areas. Members of Congress criticized the request level for SRF capitalization grants, which is $138 million below the FY2002 enacted amount. In August, the Senate Appropriations Committee approved an FY2003 funding bill for EPA that would provide $1.45 billion, $100 million more than the FY2002 level (S. 2797, S.Rept. 107-222). The House Appropriations Committee approved its version of an FY2003 funding bill, providing $1.3 billion for the clean water SRF program (H.R. 5605, H.Rept. 107-740).

Final action did not occur before the 107th Congress adjourned in November and extended into 2003, more than 5 months after the start of the fiscal year. Congress and the President reached agreement on funding levels for EPA and the other non-defense agencies in omnibus appropriations legislation, H.J.Res. 2, which the President signed on February 20 (P.L. 108-7). The enacted bill includes $1.34 billion for clean water SRF grants and $405 million more for special water infrastructure project grants to individual cities. It also provides a total of $1.14 billion for categorical state grants, including $15 million for targeted watershed grants.

FY2004

On February 3, before completion of the FY2003 appropriations, the President submitted his budget request for FY2004. It requests a total of $948 million for clean water infrastructure funds, consisting of $850 million for SRF grants and $98 million for priority projects (especially in Alaska Native Villages and in communities on the U.S.- Mexico border). As in previous years, the Administration requested no funds for congressionally earmarked project grants. The Administration responded to criticism of the request for SRF grants by saying that it reflects a commitment to fund this program at the $850 million level through FY2011. Funding at the that level, plus repayments of previous SRF loans made by states, is expected to increase the revolving levels of the overall program from $2.0 billion to $2.8 billion per year, the Administration says. The budget includes a few increases for water quality activities, including $15 million for remediation of contaminated sediments in the Great Lakes (to implement P.L. 107-303) and $5 million in additional funding (totaling $20 million) for state wetlands program development.

CONGRESSIONAL HEARINGS, REPORTS, AND DOCUMENTS

(**Note:** Congress has held more than 75 hearings on Clean Water Act and water quality issues since enactment of P.L. 100-4. Those highlighted below are a partial list of the most recent published hearings on implementation of the Act.)

U.S. Congress. House. Committee on Transportation and Infrastructure. Subcommittee on Oversight, Investigations and Emergency Management. *Total Maximum Daily Load Initiatives under the Clean Water Act.* Hearing. 106th Congress, 2nd session, July 27, 2000. Washington: GPO, 2000. 77 p. (106-106)

U.S. Congress. House. Subcommittee on Water Resources and Environment. *Improving Water Quality: States' Perspectives on the Federal Water Pollution Control Act.* Hearing. 107th Congress, 1st session, February 28, 2001. Washington: GPO, 2001. 53 p. (107-3)

—— *Water Infrastructure Needs.* Hearing. 107th Congress, 1st session, March 28, 2001. Washington: GPO, 2001. 178 p. (107-8)

—— *The National Academy of Sciences' National Research Council Report on Assessing the Scientific Basis of the Total Maximum Daily Load Approach to*

Water Quality Management. Hearing. 107th Congress, 1st session, June 28, 2001. Washington: GPO, 2001. 118 p. (107-29)

―― *The Future of the TMDL Program: How to Make TMDLs Effective Tools for Improving Water Quality.* Hearing. 107th Congress, 1st session, November 15, 2001. Washington: GPO, 2001. 34 p. (107-56)

U.S. Congress. Senate. Committee on Agriculture, Nutrition, and Forestry. *Water Quality.* Hearing. 106th Congress, 2d session, February 23, 2000. S.Hrg. 106-699. Washington: GPO, 2000. 336 p.

U.S. Congress. Senate. Committee on Environment and Public Works. *Clean Water Action Plan.* Hearings. 106th Congress, 1st session, May 13, 1999. S.Hrg. 106-389. Washington: GPO, 1999. 148 p.

U.S. Congress. Senate. Subcommittee on Fisheries, Wildlife, and Water. *Proposed Rule Changes to the TMDL and NPDES Permit Programs.* Hearings. 106th Congress, 2d session, March 1, 23, and May 18, 2000. S.Hrg. 106-971. Washington: GPO, 2000. 597 p.

―― *Water and Wastewater Infrastructure Needs.* Hearings. 107th Congress, 1st session, March 27, 2001. S.Hrg. 107-316. Washington: GPO, 2001. 141 p.

FOR ADDITIONAL READING

Goplerud, C. Peter. "Water Pollution Law: Milestones from the Past and Anticipation of the Future." *Natural Resources & Environment.* v. 10, no. 2, fall 1995. pp. 7-12.

Knopman, Debra S. and Richard A. Smith. "20 Years of the Clean Water Act, Has U.S. Water Quality Improved?" *Environment.* v. 31, no. 1, January/February 1993. pp. 16-20, 34-41.

Loeb, Penny. "Very Troubled Waters." *U.S. News & World Report,* v. 125, no. 12, September 28, 1998: 39, 41-42.

U.S. Environmental Protection Agency. *The National Water Quality Inventory: 2000 Report.* Washington, September 2002. "EPA-841-R-2-001."

―― *1996 Clean Water Needs Survey Report to Congress.* Washington, 1997. 1 vol. "EPA832/R-97-003."

U.S. General Accounting Office. *Key EPA and State Decisions Limited by Inconsistent and Incomplete Data.* (GAO/RCED-00-54) March 2000. 73 p.

Water Infrastructure: Information on Financing, Capital Planning, and Privatization. (GAO-02-764) August 2002. 79 p.

Chapter 5

CLEAN WATER ACT AND TOTAL MAXIMUM DAILY LOADS (TMDLS) OF POLLUTANTS

INTRODUCTION

Section 303(d) of the Clean Water Act requires states to identify waters that are impaired by pollution, even after application of pollution controls. For those waters, states must establish a total maximum daily load (TMDL) of pollutants to ensure that water quality standards can be attained. Implementation was dormant until states and EPA were prodded by lawsuits. The TMDL program has become controversial, in part because of requirements and costs now facing states to implement this 30-year-old provision of the law, as well as industries, cities, farmers, and others who may be required to use new pollution controls to meet TMDL requirements. In July 2000, EPA issued rules to revise and strengthen the program. The rules were widely criticized, and congressional interest has been high. The Bush Administration delayed the effective date of the rules until May 2003, to allow for additional review. In December 2002, EPA proposed to withdraw the 2000 rules while it considers initiating an entirely new rule or other options; no timetable was announced. This report will be updated.

BACKGROUND

The Clean Water Act (CWA) contains a number of complex elements of overall water quality management. Foremost is the requirement in section 303 that states establish ambient water quality standards for water bodies, consisting of the designated use or uses of a water body (e.g., recreational, public water supply, or industrial water supply) and the water quality criteria which are necessary to protect the use or uses. Through permitting, states or the Environmental Protection Agency (EPA) impose wastewater discharge limits on individual industrial and municipal facilities to ensure that water quality standards are attained. However, Congress recognized in the Act that, in many cases, pollution controls implemented by industry and cities would be insufficient, due to pollutant contributions from other unregulated sources.

Under section 303(d) of the Act, states must identify lakes, rivers, and streams for which wastewater discharge limits are not stringent enough to achieve established water quality standards, after implementation of technology-based controls by industrial and municipal dischargers. For each of these waterbodies, a state is required to set a total maximum daily load (TMDL) of pollutants at a level that ensures that applicable water quality standards can be attained and maintained. A TMDL sets the maximum amount of pollution a waterbody can receive without violating water quality standards, including a margin of safety. If a state fails to do this, the Environmental Protection Agency (EPA) is required to develop a priority list for the state and make its own TMDL determination. A TMDL is both a planning process for attaining water quality standards and a quantitative assessment of problems, pollution sources, and pollutant reductions needed to restore and protect a river, stream, or lake. TMDLs may address all pollution sources, including point sources such as municipal sewage or industrial plant discharges; nonpoint sources, such as runoff from roads, farm fields, and forests; and naturally occurring sources, such as runoff from undisturbed lands.

The TMDL itself does not establish new regulatory controls on sources of pollution. However, when TMDLs are established, municipal and industrial wastewater treatment plants may be required to install new pollution control technology. States and EPA enforce the TMDLs through revisions to existing permits which include the pollutant limits and a schedule for compliance. For waters impaired by nonpoint source runoff, because there are no federal controls over these sources under the Clean Water Act, the primary implementation measures are state-run nonpoint source management programs coupled with state, local, and federal land management programs and authorities and financial assistance programs. For example, farmers and ranchers may be asked to use alternative methods in their operations to prevent fertilizers and pesticides from reaching streams. States may require cities to manage or control runoff from streets.

IMPLEMENTATION

TMDLs are one element of water quality management programs conducted by states to implement the CWA. Other activities include standard setting, monitoring, permitting, and enforcement. Integrating them with the TMDL program is difficult because of factors such as different program purposes and schedules. Most states have lacked the resources to do TMDL analyses, which involve complex assessment of point and nonpoint sources in order to ascribe and quantify environmental effects for particular discharge sources. Baseline water quality monitoring data for the analyses (to identify impaired waters and pollution sources) is limited. EPA has both been reluctant to intervene in the states and has also lacked resources to do so itself. Thus, there had been little implementation of the provision which was enacted in 1972. Only in 1992 did EPA issue regulations requiring states every 2 years to list waters that do not attain water quality standards and establish TMDLs to restore water quality.

Responding to the failure of both states and EPA to meet these requirements, however, environmental groups have filed 40 lawsuits in 38 states in the last few years. Environmentalists see implementation of section 303(d) as important both to achieving the overall goals and objectives of the Act and pressuring EPA and states to address nonpoint and other sources which are responsible for many water quality impairments nationwide but have not been controlled up to this point. Of the suits tried or settled to date, 22 have resulted in court orders requiring expeditious development of TMDLs by states or EPA.

The TMDL litigation falls into five general categories, according to EPA: (1) situations in which a state has failed to perform any section 303(d) activities; (2) situations in which a state has engaged in some but insufficient activities to implement section 303(d); (3) challenges to EPA's listing of impaired waters, TMDL approval, or EPA's promulgation of TMDLs; (4) situations in which plaintiffs are using TMDL requirements to achieve other CWA objectives, such as forcing improved water quality monitoring programs; and (5) challenges to the substance or content of TMDLs.[1]

Because of the lawsuits and existing requirements of the law, in August 1997, EPA issued a policy which for the first time called on states to develop long-term schedules for implementing TMDLs. Under that policy, EPA directed states to

---

[1] For a summary of TMDL litigation by state, see information on EPA's Web site: [http://www.epa.gov/owow/tmdl/lawsuit1.html].

establish TMDLs in order to meet water quality standards within 8 to 13 years.[2] Development of TMDLs is being initiated at an increasing pace (states and EPA have established about 7,800 since 1996), but most remain to be completed. The most recent state 303(d) lists, submitted in 1998, identified over 20,000 waterbodies as not meeting water quality standards, and EPA estimates that as many as 40,000 TMDLs may need to be developed for these waters.

In August 1999, EPA proposed revisions to the TMDL regulations to clarify and strengthen the program. The key proposed changes included: a new requirement for a more comprehensive list of impaired and threatened waterbodies; a new requirement that states, territories and authorized Indian tribes establish and submit schedules for establishing TMDLs; a new requirement that the listing methodologies be more specific, subject to public review, and submitted to EPA; clarification that TMDLs include 10 specific elements; a new requirement for an implementation plan in TMDLs; and new public participation requirements.

EPA's proposal had few strong supporters, for varying reasons. States, which would be directly affected by the proposal, criticized the burdens that new requirements would place on them. They are concerned that they lack the resources to meet tight deadlines for developing and implementing TMDLs. Further, states say that TMDLs should not necessarily be prioritized over other elements of existing water quality management programs. Industry groups are greatly concerned about impacts of new pollution control requirements. But, municipal and industrial point source groups urge states and EPA to ensure that TMDL requirements do not fall disproportionately on their discharges, while possibly failing to address nonpoint source contributions to impaired waters. Farm groups and others with nonpoint discharges question EPA's authority to include nonpoint source pollution in the TMDL program. The forestry industry vigorously criticized potential impacts of the proposal. Environmentalists, who support the need for a stronger and more comprehensive TMDL program, objected to the lengthy time periods in the proposal before water quality improvements are likely to occur. They criticize the lack of aggressive implementation of a program that has existed in the law since 1972.

Congressional interest has been high: by the time the final rule was signed in July 2000, 13 congressional hearings had been held, and six legislative proposals

---

[2] This is a longer time frame than has been mandated as a result of some of the TMDL litigation. The schedules for TMDLs in 2 lawsuits concluded by consent decrees and settlement agreements range from 4 years to 20 years; most call for a 10-year development schedule.

to modify the Clean Water Act or delay the rule had been introduced.[3] EPA attempted to respond to the widespread criticism and signal flexibility on some of the most contentious points. While the revised rule was undergoing final review, Congress adopted a provision in H.R. 4425, the FY2001 Military Constructions/FY2000 Urgent Supplemental Appropriations Bill, stating that no funds may be used in FY2000 or FY2001 to "make a final determination on or implement any new rule relative to" the August 1999 proposal. Because President Clinton intended to sign H.R. 4425 into law but opposed the TMDL provision, the Administration accelerated its review, allowing the EPA Administrator to sign it before President Clinton signed the appropriations bill on July 13 (P.L. 106-246). In the final rule, EPA acknowledged Congress' action in H.R. 4425 and delayed the effective date of the rule's changes until Oct. 31, 2001. The text of the final rule was published on July 13, 2000.[4]

The final rule built on the current TMDL regulatory program and added details, specific requirements, and deadlines that require states to implement plans to clean up polluted waters. It retained the basic elements of the 1999 proposal for more comprehensive identification of impaired waters, schedules and minimum elements for TMDLs, and new public participation requirements. For some interested parties, what was most of interest was what was not included in the final rule. EPA dropped several provisions that were most controversial, including some potentially affecting agriculture and forestry. The Bush Administration announced in October 2001 that it would delay the effective date of the rule until May 2003, to allow for further review. That announcement came after a federal court granted the Administration's request for a similar 18-month suspension of litigation which is challenging the regulation (nearly a dozen interest groups have sued EPA over various parts of the TMDL rule).

In December 2002, EPA proposed to withdraw the 2000 rule while it considers initiating an entirely new rule or other options. Officials said that additional time beyond May is needed to decide whether and how to revise the program and that allowing the rule to take effect would disrupt the ongoing review. No further timetable was announced. In the interim, current program

---

[3] During the 106th Congress, hearings were held by the full committee or subcommittees of the House Agriculture Committee, House Transportation and Infrastructure Committee, Senate Agriculture, Nutrition and Forestry Committee, and Senate Environment and Public Works Committee. Legislative proposals included H.R. 3609, H.R. 3625, H.R. 4502, S. 2041, S. 2139, and S. 2417. H.R. 4922 was introduced after EPA issued the final revised rule.

[4] U.S. Environmental Protection Agency. "Revisions to the Water Quality Planning and Management Regulation and Revisions to the National Pollutant Discharge Elimination System Program in Support of Revisions to the Water Quality Planning and Management Regulation; Final Rules." 65 *Federal Register* No. 135, July 13, 2000, pp. 43586-43670.

requirements under the 1992 regulations and courtsanctioned TMDL schedules remain in place. Stakeholders now are urging EPA to adopt different strategies. Environmentalists say that, short of retaining the 2000 rule, the best action would be to leave the 1992 rules in place, because, though flawed, those rules are preferable to a new rule that might weaken the program. States and many industries are urging EPA to develop a new rule with greater implementation and enforcement flexibility than either the 2000 rule or existing regulations.

ISSUES FOR CONGRESS

A number of issues and options for Congress are apparent.

- **Do nothing at this time.** EPA had hoped that its regulatory proposals would achieve improvements to the TMDL program and not require legislative changes to the Clean Water Act, since the outcome of the legislative process is uncertain. EPA also hoped that modifications of the 1999 proposal which it included in the final rule would lessen criticism and perhaps deter congressional action. If the 2000 rule is withdrawn, as now proposed, stakeholders will carefully analyze future EPA decisions.

- **Strengthen the current program.** Environmentalists have long sought to strengthen the program, and some favor amending the Act to: impose clear deadlines on states and EPA to carry out section 303(d), as there are no statutory deadlines in current law; make clear that EPA has a nondiscretionary duty to act if a state fails to do so and define what EPA actions and/or penalties would follow; and ensure that states periodically update lists of impaired waters, so that TMDL implementation evolves as water quality conditions change.

- **Provide flexibility or limit the program.** The need for flexibility to develop and implement TMDLs is a key issue for states and industry. Many favor policies that would not commit them to specific timeframes for establishing and implementing TMDLs, but instead call for schedules to reflect the availability of sound science and resources. Water quality data are so limited, particularly concerning nonpoint sources, that many fear that TMDL decisions will be based on unsound information and will impose unneeded or inappropriate control mandates. The General Accounting Office reported in 2000 that inconsistent monitoring, data collection, and listing procedures used by states to identify impaired waters have hindered efforts to develop effective TMDL programs (*Water Quality: Key EPA and State Decisions Limited by Inconsistent and Incomplete Data*, GAO-00-54).

- **Clarify the program's impact on nonpoint sources.** Nonpoint sources (both urban and rural) cause or contribute to water quality impairments throughout the United States. Section 303(d) currently does not specify whether TMDLs should cover nonpoint sources, but EPA's long-standing interpretation is that sources of polluted runoff should be included, along with point sources. EPA's interpretation has been upheld in a key court case (*Pronsolino v. Marcus*, 91 F.Supp.2d 1337 (N.D.Cal Mar. 30, 2000) *aff'd, Pronsolino v. Nastri*, CA9, No. 00-16026, 5/31/02). To limit TMDL implementation only to point sources would likely impose disproportionate requirements on cities and industries, which have been the traditional focus of the CWA's regulatory requirements. The 2000 rule explicitly included nonpoint source-impaired waters in the program. Farming and forestry groups contend that other non-regulatory CWA programs are directed at nonpoint source pollution, and they were concerned that EPA intends to regulate their activities through permits. They favor excluding nonpoint sources from TMDLs, so that they do not bear the costs of implementation and pollution controls. EPA clarified in the final rule its understanding that it lacks regulatory authority over nonpoint sources and only can influence their activities through use of grants and funding.

- **Consider the resource question.** Both EPA and states face significant financial and technical challenges, and costs of the TMDL rule have been one of the most controversial issues. In 2000, the Agency projected that the incremental cost of the rule to states will be about $23 million per year, but states believe that costs will be higher and that assistance to states should triple to meet their increased needs. The Bush Administration has requested only limited budget increases in FY2003 or FY2004 for EPA and state TMDL activities.

- **Further study and analysis.** EPA's FY2001 appropriation bill, P.L. 106-377, required studies by the National Academy of Sciences (NAS) and EPA on the scientific basis of the program and on the costs to states and businesses of implementing the TMDL rules. The NAS report, issued in

June 2001, concluded that scientific knowledge exists to move forward with the program but recommended changes to improve implementation. EPA's current review of the 2000 rule is at least partly to consider how to respond to those recommendations. EPA issued a draft report on TMDL program costs in August 2001, estimating that average annual costs to states and EPA of developing TMDLs could be $63-$69 million, while implementation costs for pollutant sources could be between $900 million and $4.3 billion per year, depending on states' actions.

Finally, the recent attention to the TMDL program raises some challenging questions about the quality of the nation's surface waters, those subject to the Clean Water Act. After 30 years of implementing the law, EPA and states acknowledge that a substantial portion of the nation's waters still are impaired or threatened by pollution. The most recent national inventory of water quality reported that nearly 40% of surveyed water bodies remain too polluted for fishing, swimming, and other designated uses.[5] Yet those numbers only represent rivers, streams, and lakes actually surveyed by state monitoring programs – typically about one-third of all waters. The TMDL assessments developed by states are yielding more precise water quality information and are identifying large numbers of stream segments which require additional measures before water quality standards are attained. Full implementation of the TMDL process is likely to inform policymakers more completely about conditions nationwide. Additional congressional oversight of these issues also is likely.

---

[5] U.S. Environmental Protection Agency. Office of Water. THE NATIONAL WATER QUALITY INVENTORY: 2000 REPORT.. Washington, September 2002. 1 vol. EPA-841-R-2-001. Report is available at: [http://www.epa.gov/305b/2000report/].

Chapter 6

THE CLEAN WATER ACT'S TMDL PROGRAM: NEWLY PRESENTED OPTIONS AND COST ESTIMATES

INTRODUCTION

Two reports requested by Congress on the Environmental Protection Agency's(EPA) controversial TMDL program have recently been released. This program, authorized by section 303(d) of the Clean Water Act, requires states to set "total maximum daily loads" (TMDLs) of pollution to ensure that pollutant-impaired waters are improved. At issue have been controversies over implementation of the existing TMDL program and regulatory revisions that EPA issued in July 2000 to strengthen it.[1] Congress mandated studies by the National Academy of Sciences (NAS) and EPA on the scientific basis of the TMDL program and on the potential costs of implementing the TMDL regulation. The NAS report was issued on June 15, 2001,and on August 3, EPA released a draft report estimating national costs of the TMDL program. EPA proposes to delay the 2000 rule until May 2003 for review and revision. This report is a brief overview of the NAS and EPA reports.

The NAS panel concluded that sufficient scientific knowledge exists to move forward with the TMDL program and that while there will always be uncertainties concerning water quality science, those uncertainties do not prevent making good decisions based on existing scientific knowledge. The TMDL process is not fundamentally flawed, the committee said, but implementation can be improved.

---

[1] For information, see CRS Report 97-831, Clean Water Act and Total Maximum DailyLoads (TMDLs) of Pollutants.

The NAS panel concluded that, using current science, EPA and states can immediately make several changes to the TMDL program that will improve it. To address uncertainties in identifying impaired waters, the panel recommends that identification be a two-step process, not a single process as it is now. Using available data, waters suspected of being impaired would be placed on a preliminary list. Then, using more complete assessment, the water body would be moved either to a "no impairment" list or to an action list for further structured investigation and TMDL development and for review of the underlying water quality standard. The panel also recommends the use of adaptive implementation for TMDLs. In many cases, water quality problems and solutions are obvious and should proceed without complex analysis. In other cases, solutions are more complex and may require something like phased or iterative implementation.

In its report, EPA estimates that the total cost to states and EPA to develop 36,000 TMDLs for the 22,000 rivers, streams, lakes and coastal waters known to be impaired to be about $1 billion. Nearly all of that total is associated with requirements of the existing program, not the 2000 revisions. Costs of developing TMDLs over the next 15 years are estimated to be $63-$69 million annually.

The EPA report also examined potential costs to the public and private sectors of implementing TMDLs. EPA estimates that implementation costs for pollutant sources could be between $900 million and $4.3 billion annually, depending on states' actions in allocating pollutant load reductions and distributing costs among different stakeholders to achieve a water quality goal. Industrial and municipal point sources will incur most of those costs, due to higher per pound abatement costs, even though nonpoint sources affect more than 90% of impaired waters.

BACKGROUND

Under section 303(d) of the Clean Water Act, states must identify lakes, rivers, and streams for which wastewater discharge limits are not stringent enough to achieve established water quality standards, after implementation of technology-based controls by industrial and municipal dischargers. For each of these water bodies, a state is required to set a TMDL of pollutants at a level that ensures that applicable water quality standards can be attained and maintained. A TMDL sets the maximum amount of pollution a waterbody can receive without violating water quality standards, including a margin of safety. If a state fails to do this, the EPA is required to develop a priority list of impaired waters for the state and make its own TMDL determination.

The TMDL itself does not establish new regulatory controls on sources of pollution. However, when TMDLs are established, municipal and industrial wastewater treatment plants may be required to install new pollution control technology. States and EPA enforce the TMDLs through revisions to existing permits which include the pollutant limits and a schedule for compliance. For waters impaired by nonpoint source runoff (such as from roads, farm fields, and forests), because there are no federal controls over these sources under the Clean Water Act, the primary implementation measures are state-run management programs coupled with state, local, and federal land management programs and authorities and financial assistance programs. For example, farmers and ranchers may be asked to use alternative methods in their operations to prevent fertilizers and pesticides from reaching rivers; current federal law cannot compel them to do so, however. Cities, which are subject to permits and the Act's enforcement mechanisms, may be required by states to manage or control runoff from streets.

Congress enacted section 303(d) in 1972 (P.L. 92-500), but it had languished for many years until more than 40 lawsuits were brought challenging the lack of implementation by states and EPA. Environmentalists see implementation of section 303(d) as important both to achieving the overall goals and objectives of the Act and pressuring EPA and states to address sources of pollution which are responsible for many water quality impairments nationwide but have not been controlled up to this point. In July 2000, EPA issued regulations to revise the existing TMDL rules (last revised in 1992), in order to strengthen the program and to halt the litigation.

EPA's 2000 TMDL regulation has had few strong supporters, for varying reasons. States, which would be directly affected by the proposal, criticized the burdens that new requirements would place on them. They are concerned that they lack the resources to meet tight deadlines to develop and implement TMDLs. Further, states say that TMDLs should not necessarily be prioritized over other elements of existing water quality management programs. Industry groups are greatly concerned about impacts of new pollution control requirements. But, municipal and industrial point source groups urge states and EPA to ensure that TMDL requirements do not fall disproportionately on their discharges, while possibly failing to address nonpoint source contributions to impaired waters. Farm groups and others associated with nonpoint discharges question EPA's authority to include nonpoint source pollution in the TMDL program. The forestry industry vigorously criticized potential impacts of the proposed rule on its activities. A number of environmentalists, who support the need for a stronger and more comprehensive TMDL program, objected to the lengthy time periods in the rule before water quality improvements are likely to occur. They criticize the lack of aggressive implementation of a program that has existed in the law since 1972.

Because of the continuing controversies, when the revised rule was issued in July 2000, EPA delayed the effective date of the rule's changes until October 2001.[2] In the interim, current program requirements under existing regulations and court-sanctioned TMDL schedules remain in place (more than 20 lawsuits have resulted in court orders or settlements requiring expeditious development of TMDLs). Subsequently, Congress called for two studies by the NAS and EPA that would provide policymakers with added information about the TMDL program. Report language accompanying the Senate version of EPA's FY2001 appropriation act (S.Rept. 106-410), P.L. 106-377, specified the two studies. First, it called for the NAS to "review the quality of science used to develop and implement TMDLs" by evaluating the information required to identify sources of pollutants, allocate pollutant reductions, and the availability and reliability of information for these activities. Second, it called for EPA to conduct a comprehensive assessment of the potential state resources needed for TMDL development and implementation and an estimate of the annual costs to the private sector due to TMDL implementation. Also, EPA was directed to prepare an analysis of the monitoring data needed for the TMDL program, in view of criticisms by the General Accounting Office[3] and others about data gaps for assessing impaired waters and developing and implementing TMDLs.

In response, the NAS issued its report on TMDL science on June 15, and EPA issued a draft national cost report in early August. EPA is taking public comment on its report until December 7 and expects to issue a report with updated information later, after some data are refined.

On August 9, the Bush Administration formally proposed to delay the October 2001 effective date for 18 months (until May 2003) to allow EPA officials time to review the 2000 rule and the recent NAS report. The Administration also is seeking a similar stay of litigation which is challenging the regulation (nearly a dozen interest groups sued EPA over various parts of the TMDL rule in American Farm Bureau Federation v. Whitman, D.C. Cir., No. 00-1320 and consolidated cases). The court has not yet acted on EPA's request. A House Transportation and Infrastructure subcommittee held a hearing on the NAS report on June 28, and additional congressional oversight on this and other TMDL issues is likely.

---

[2] For additional information, see CRS Report RL30611, EPA's TMDL Program: Highlights of the Final Revised Rule.

[3] U.S. General Accounting Office. Water Quality: Key EPA and State Decisions Limited by Inconsistent and Incomplete Data.GAO/RCED-00-54. March 2000. 73 p.

THE NAS REPORT

The NAS report, examining the role of science in the TMDL program, was issued June 15.[4] The work of the eight-member panel focused on the existing program, not the regulatory changes issued in 2000, but the report states that many of its recommendations apply to either the current or the revised program.

The report contains analysis for all parties in the TMDL debate, both supporters and critics. The panel concluded that sufficient scientific knowledge exists to move forward with the TMDL program and that while there will always be uncertainties concerning water quality science, those uncertainties do not prevent making good decisions based on existing scientific knowledge. The TMDL process is not fundamentally flawed, the committee concluded, but implementation can be improved. Its report targets recommendation in two areas: (1) those where science can and should play a role and (2) barriers (regulatory and otherwise) to the use of science.

The NAS panel also concluded that, using current science, EPA and states can immediately make several changes to the TMDL program that will improve it. These recommendations, the committee said, involve changes in the techniques used in the TMDL process, not development of new techniques. For example, the committee notes that EPA requires that TMDLs contain a "margin of safety" factor to protect water quality by reflecting uncertainty. However, EPA allows the margin of safety to be arbitrarily chosen by states, resulting in a variable level of protection. Thus, the committee recommends using existing techniques to base the margin of safety on an explicit calculation of uncertainty.

The committee also observes that many states have not used well-designed monitoring programs with appropriate statistical testing to diagnose violations of water quality standards. Thus, it is believed that some or many water bodies have been mis-diagnosed - some as incorrectly in violation of standards, and some not yet identified, although they truly are in violation.

To address uncertainties in the current process of listing impaired waters, the panel recommends that listing be a two-step process, not a single process as it is now. Using available, even if limited, data, waters suspected of being impaired would be placed on a preliminary list. Then, using more complete assessment to reduce the uncertainty about condition, the water body would be moved either to an action list or to a "no impairment" list, as appropriate. Waters moved to an action list would be candidates for further analytically structured investigation and

---

[4] National Research Council. Water Science and Technology Board. Assessing the TMDL Approach to Water Quality Management. June 2001. 122 p.

TMDL development and for review of the underlying water quality standard. Models are important throughout these steps, the panel said, but do not eliminate the need for informed decision-making.

A potentially controversial part of the committee's report is discussion of reviewing ambient standards for waters on a state's action list. To some, this recommendation suggests that the result would be weakening of water quality control efforts, especially if states were to conclude that originally set standards are unattainable because control costs are too high, and therefore that standards should be revised and downgraded. The report observes that the TMDL process is primarily a measurement process and as such is significantly impacted by the setting of water quality standards. Water quality standards consist of two parts: a designated use, which is a narrative description of the goal of the standard such as protecting human contact recreation; and a scientific criterion that measures whether the designated use is being achieved. The NAS panel acknowledges that there may be cases where a more carefully defined designated use is appropriate. For example, rather than stating that the water body needs to be "fishable," the designated use would describe a desired fish population, such as salmon, that the water body is expected to support. Appropriate use designation is a policy decision, the panel said, but technical analysis can inform the decision.

Water quality criteria, including biological, chemical, and physical measures, define the types of data to be collected and assessed in order to determine achievement of a designated use. The panel recommends that criteria chosen to measure use attainment should be logically linked to the designated use and should be more extensive than criteria typically used by states today. More than one criterion may be necessary for precisely determining causes and sources of impairments. The panel suggests that the goal of water quality monitoring should be a comprehensive set of measured parameters to provide different and complementary types of information about the source and extent of impairment.

In a similar vein to its recommendation for two-step listing of impaired waters, the NAS panel recommends the use of adaptive implementation for TMDLs. In many cases, the report said, water quality problems and solutions are obvious and should proceed without complex analysis. In other cases, solutions are more complex and require something like phased or iterative implementation. Such an adaptive approach, which would allow taking low cost/high certainty actions first, then monitoring and scientific reassessment of next steps, also differs from the current program which essentially requires states to commit to implementing a series of actions when a TMDL is developed. The adaptive implementation concept is controversial with some environmental advocates, concerned about prolonged delays in achieving water quality standards. But proponents argue that it could lead to better and more cost-effective decisions.

Finally, the NAS panel observes that decisions on allocating reductions in pollutant loadings among sources first and foremost are policy questions because the different combinations among point sources, nonpoint sources, or other water quality management opportunities will have a different total cost and different levels of perceived fairness. Science can play a role, however, by determining when possible actions across sources are equivalent, in terms of assessing ambient water out comes and recognizing the relative uncertainty of different actions.

The NAS concludes by noting without specific recommendations three underlying policy issues that need to be resolved.

- Because the water quality standards that underlie listing a water as impaired often are weak and predictions about what actions will affect a designated use are uncertain, there needs to be accommodation for growth and change in watersheds as implementation proceeds until a designated use has been achieved.

- Distributing the costs and regulatory burdens of the TMDL process in a manner that is deemed equitable by all stakeholders (including point sources subject to permits and enforcement, as well as unregulated point sources) is critical to the program's success.

- If adaptive implementation is endorsed, it may require changed roles for states and EPA. States may be required to assume more responsibility for TMDLs, while EPA may need to elevate the level of its oversight from individual TMDLs and water segments to the overall program.

Criticism of the TMDL program often focuses (and sometimes inappropriately) on the quality of data and information, rather than these issues, the panel stated.

THE EPA REPORT

EPA's report on costs of the TMDL program, issued as a draft on August 3,[5] was stimulated in part by controversy about EPA's previous estimate of the cost

---

[5] U.S. Environmental Protection Agency. Office of Water. The National Costs of the Total Maximum Daily Load Program (Draft Report). EPA 841-D-01-003. August 2001. See[http://www.epa.gov/owow/tmdl]

impact of the program. EPA estimated in July 2000 that the regulatory revisions issued at that time will impose annual incremental costs totaling $22.88 million on states, territories, and Indian Tribes that implement the section 303(d) program, above baseline requirements of the existing program. By that estimate, the rule did not require a detailed analysis of costs, benefits, and alternatives, as is required by the Unfunded Mandates Reform Act of 1995, if a regulation includes a federal mandate that would result in expenditure by state and local governments or the private sector of more than $100 million in any one year. States believed that EPA had greatly underestimated costs of the program. Many were critical that in evaluating its proposal to revise the existing program, EPA had focused solely on the incremental costs of program revisions. The Agency believed that it was only necessary to estimate the costs of changes beyond the base program, since those requirements have existed for some time.

EPA also was faulted for not estimating possible impacts on small governments, small businesses such as farmers and landowners, or larger businesses. EPA explained in the July 2000 rule that, because the rule does not directly apply to any discharger, including small entities, and since impacts on non-government entities are indirect, the Agency did not have to prepare a regulatory flexibility analysis, as would be required by the Regulatory Flexibility Act if the rule imposes substantial economic impact on small entities. Impacts on the private sector and local governments would flow from requirements already established by section 303(d) and the states' water quality standards, EPA said, not directly from the revised TMDL rule.

Developing TMDLs: Costs to States

To develop a national estimate of the cost of developing TMDLs, EPA used information on the number of needed TMDLs,[6] unit development costs, the complexity of different TMDLs, and the potential for efficiencies through TMDL coordination. Based on this information, in its August 2001 report, EPA estimates the total cost to develop 36,000 TMDLs for the 22,000 rivers, streams, lakes, and coastal waters known to be impaired to be about $1 billion. The total cost could be lower or higher by about 15%, depending on states' efficiency in coordinating the development of TMDLs.

The Agency projects that the costs to states, territories, Indian Tribes, and EPA of developing TMDLs over the next 15 years will be from $63-69 million

---

[6] These data were based on the most recent (1998) lists of impaired water submitted by states, as required by section 303(d). States and EPA have developed about 2,400 TMDLs so far.

annually. EPA expects that states will increase the number of TMDLs developed each year from about 1,000 per year in 2000 to about 2,550 by 2005 and annually thereafter, thus increasing costs from about $30 million in 2000 to about $68-75 million in 2005 and annually thereafter until 2015. Average costs per TMDL will range from $26,000 to over $500,000, depending on the number of TMDLs, their level of difficulty, and the extent to which impaired waters are clustered together, thus affording administrative efficiencies.

Significantly, EPA states in the draft report that nearly all of the $1 billion total cost is associated with requirements of the existing TMDL program. The July 2000 rule added a new development task for states (preparing an implementation plan) and increased requirements for public participation. However, EPA estimates that these additional requirements account for less than 10% of the total costs of developing TMDLs.

EPA also estimates that the cost to states of identifying and listing impaired waters are the same under the existing rule and the July 2000 rule - $4.5 million total on a discounted basis over 15 years - because the new rule's additional requirements are more than offset by changing the listing cycle from two years to four years.

The recent NAS committee report extensively addresses monitoring needs in connection with listing of impaired waters and TMDL development. EPA's report separately estimates monitoring costs associated with the TMDL program. Based on a limited survey of nine states' existing monitoring programs and TMDL workloads, EPA estimates that the incremental cost of monitoring for TMDL development is $17.3 million annually nationwide. (The report does not estimate baseline costs for monitoring.) The Agency states that there is wide variation across states in the degree to which additional monitoring is needed for TMDL development, since various monitoring programs exist to meet different scientific and regulatory purposes.

Implementing TMDLs: Costs to Pollutant Sources

As noted above, the July 2000 rule did not discuss potential costs to the public and private sectors of implementing TMDLs developed by states and EPA. The Agency's analytic approach to developing such a projection was to estimate the implementation costs for all of the nation's impaired water bodies by employing a series of simplifying assumptions about what all TMDLs will require of relevant sources. Analysts used a small sample of 15 case studies to shed light on assumptions, but not as a basis for projecting the national cost of TMDLs. The

August 2001 report presents three broad scenarios of these costs, attempting to reflect the fact that neither the law nor regulations prescribe how states shall allocate load reductions among sources that discharge pollutants contributing to a pollutant. TMDLs may address all pollution sources, including point sources such as municipal sewage or industrial plant discharges; nonpoint sources, such as runoff from roads, farm fields, and forests; and naturally occurring sources, such as runoff from undisturbed lands. This point echoes the observation in the NAS panel's report that allocating pollutant load reductions is primarily a policy decision on how to distribute costs among different stakeholders to achieve a water quality goal. EPA states that, until more TMDLs are developed, analysts do not know what sources will be found responsible for each impairment and what degree of load reduction will be required of sources; thus, the cost estimates in EPA's report are subject to substantial uncertainty.

- **The "Least Flexible TMDL Program" Scenario.** Under this scenario, all pollutant sources, point and nonpoint, that contribute an impairment pollutant to a listed water would be addressed in isolation from others and would be required to adopt additional controls. EPA believes that this scenario is unlikely because it over-controls sources and imposes unreasonable costs because controls would be implemented without flexibility to all contributing sources. Annual costs to sources under this scenario are estimated to be $1.8 to $4.3 billion. Under this scenario, half or more of the costs would be incurred by point sources ($1.1 to $2.2 billion annually), which generally incur higher per pound abatement costs than do nonpoint sources, even though point sources affect only about one-quarter of the impaired waters while nonpoint sources either alone or in combination with others affect more than 90%.

- **The "Moderately Cost-Effective TMDL Program" Scenario.** This scenario describes EPA's assumption of how TMDLs will normally be developed and implemented. In it, a finer calculation is made than in the previous scenario to determine which sources will need to reduce their loads and by how much. Consequently, in many cases, depending on severity of the impairment, from a few to many of the sources may not have to reduce their discharges. Annual costs to sources under this scenario are estimated to be $1.0 to $3.4 billion. As under the first scenario, half or more of the costs could be incurred by point sources ($812 million to $1.6 billion).

- **The "More Cost-Effective TMDL Program" Scenario.** This scenario describes a situation in which states attempt to reduce aggregate costs by assigning responsibility for achieving most of the desired load reduction to sources that have relatively low costs of achieving load reductions. It reflects savings that could result from shifting some point source control responsibilities to nonpoint sources (for example, if trading is allowed after the allocation of needed load reductions). Even so, point sources may still incur the majority of implementation costs, according to EPA. Annual costs to sources under this scenario are estimated to be $906 million to $3.2 billion; costs incurred by point sources are projected to be $625 million to $1.3 billion.

EPA notes that the high-end estimate of more than $4 billion to fully implement cleanup of impaired waters in the worst-case scenario is "a fraction of current national expenditures for clean water."[7] Public and private expenditures for water pollution control in 1994 (the most recent year for which national data were reported by the Bureau of Economic Analysis, Department of Commerce) were $42.4 billion.[8]

EPA also estimated costs for management measures likely to be adopted by four types of nonpoint sources - agricultural land (including crop land, pasture land, and range land), animal feeding operations, silviculture, and on-site wastewater treatment systems (i.e., septic systems). The Agency estimates that the preponderance of costs to nonpoint sources (from 80% to 90%) would result from utilizing best management practices (BMPs) on agricultural crop land, while only 2% to 5% of costs would affect silviculture nonpoint sources, for example. Cropland BMPs include measures to limit erosion such as conservation tillage, contour farming, use of filter strips or other vegetative cover to catch pollutants, rotational planting, or improved timing of nutrient and pesticide application.

EPA did not, however, estimate costs for achieving load reductions from several difficult-to-analyze nonpoint source types, including mineral extraction, atmospheric deposition, and contaminated in-stream sediments because of insufficient data to estimate cleanup costs . EPA estimates that these source types account for about14% of all impaired river miles and 22% of impaired lake acreage. Some can entail high mitigation costs, but if economic impacts are

---

[7] U.S. Environmental Protection Agency. "EPA Estimates Costs of Clean Water TMDL Program." Press release, Aug. 3, 2001. See [http://www.epa.gov/owow/tmdl/draftdocs.html]

[8] Vogan, Christine R. "Pollution Abatement and Control Expenditures, 1972-94." Survey of Current Business. September 1996: 48-67.

excessive, states may evaluate the need to revise an underlying water quality standard giving rise to the TMDL.

EPA asserts that in many cases BMPs implemented through TMDLs will result in substantial savings that offset some portion of the BMP costs - for example, if improved nutrient management yields savings to farmers from otherwise purchasing commercial fertilizers. However, EPA did not incorporate estimates of national savings that might result from BMPs because of the great uncertainty about such savings. Analysts hope to gather more data on these questions.

Estimating the Unknown Part of the TMDL Problem

According to EPA, water bodies known to be impaired include approximately 300,000 miles of rivers and coastal shoreline and approximately 5 million acres of lakes. Because water quality monitoring programs have assessed only about one-third of all waters, this quantity represents about one-third of all waters whose quality has been assessed, or about 10% of all waters nationwide. Approximately 75% of the U.S. population lives within 10 miles of an impaired waterbody.

The EPA report also addresses the question of how extensive the problem of impaired waters might be if 100% of waters were being monitored and assessed, rather than approximately one-third. EPA acknowledges that more impaired waterbodies needing TMDLs likely will be identified, as assessment and monitoring efforts expand. However, the Agency cites reasons why it believes that far fewer water quality problems will be identified than in the recent past. First, EPA believes that states have generally focused monitoring on known problems, thus most impairments have already been identified. Second, many of the unassessed areas are unlikely to be impaired (many are located in pristine areas, for example). Third, EPA believes that future impairment of currently assessed waters (i.e., waters that now are threatened to become impaired by new pollutant causes) is not likely to be significant and could add from 20% to 30% more needed TMDLs. At the same time, EPA believes that the total TMDL workload will decrease as currently-identified TMDLs are developed and standards are achieved, and waters erroneously identified because of insufficient data are de-listed. Over a lengthy period of time (nine listing cycles, or through2038), a total of 9,000 additional TMDLs, or about 25% of the current workload, are projected to be required.

CONCLUSION

It is unclear for now how the information in these two new reports will affect debate about the TMDL program. As described above, EPA has proposed delaying the effective date of the July 2000 rule to review that rule. The outcome of that process will not be known for some time, but Agency sources have said that officials will meet with stakeholders later in the fall in hope of proposing changes by spring2002.[9] The NAS panel's recommendations, such as for adaptive implementation of TMDLs, may assist EPA; states and others have previously also suggested phased implementation. On the cost side, EPA's draft report shows what many stakeholders already recognize - that total costs to meet the Clean Water Act's water quality goals are high, probably very high. Revising the July 2000 rule may not substantially alter that fact. At issue is evaluating both potential costs and benefits.

EPA officials are reported to believe that delaying the 2000 rule will allow the Agency to put in place a workable program reflecting agreement among diverse stakeholders. Based on past controversies, however, it is likely that agreement will continue to be difficult to achieve.

---

[9] Bureau of National Affairs, Inc. "EPA to Accept Comments on 18-Month Delay of Effective Date for Impaired Waters Rule." DAILY ENVIRONMENT REPORT. Aug. 9, 2001.No. 153: A-1.

Chapter 7

CLEAN WATER ACT ISSUES

INTRODUCTION

Prospects for legislative initiatives to comprehensively amend the Clean Water Act (CWA) have stalled for some time over whether and exactly how to change the law, and Congress has recently focused legislative attention on narrow bills to extend or modify selected CWA programs, rather than taking up comprehensive proposals.

The 107th Congress enacted a bill authorizing funding to clean up contaminated sediments in the Great Lakes (P.L. 107-303). However, the most prominent water quality issue concerned financial assistance for municipal wastewater treatment projects. House and Senate committees approved bills to reauthorize the Act's wastewater infrastructure funding program, but no further action occurred. This issue is likely to predominate in the 108th Congress, as well. At issue is how the federal government will assist states and cities in meeting needs to rebuild, repair, and upgrade wastewater treatment plants, especially in light of capital costs which are projected to be as much as $390 billion over the next two decades.

Several other Clean Water Act issues are likely to receive congressional attention, through oversight hearings and possibly in legislative proposals. Among the topics of interest is whether and how the Administration will revise the current program for restoration of pollution-impaired waters (the Total Maximum Daily Load, or TMDL program), in view of controversy over regulatory changes made during the Clinton Administration and continuing disagreement among states, cities, industry, and environmental advocates about program effectiveness and efficiency.

Programs that regulate activities in wetlands, especially CWA Section 404, have been criticized by landowners for intruding on private land-use decisions and imposing excessive economic burdens. Environmentalists view these programs as essential for maintaining the health of wetland ecosystems. These groups are concerned about a 2001 Supreme Court decision that narrowed regulatory protection of wetlands, as well as recent administrative actions which they believe will likewise diminish protection.

Also of interest are water pollution problems due to waste discharges from large animal feeding operations, termed Confined Animal Feeding Operations (CAFOs). The 108th Congress may examine details of revised clean water rules for management of CAFO waste issued by EPA in December 2002 and overall efforts to address animal waste management problems.

Early indications suggest that the 108th Congress, like the 107th Congress, will focus on water infrastructure funding legislation. However, it is expected that the key authorizing committees (House Transportation and Infrastructure and Senate Environment and Public Works) will address other legislative priorities such as reauthorization of surface transportation funding and water resources development programs before considering Clean Water Act legislation.

MOST RECENT DEVELOPMENTS

Water infrastructure funding legislation is expected to be a priority in the 108th Congress because of recent estimates by the Environmental Protection Agency that as much as $390 billion will be needed over the next two decades to rebuild, repair, and upgrade the nation's wastewater treatment plants. Several bills have been introduced in the 108th Congress, but no further action has occurred. In the 107th Congress, House and Senate committees approved bills to authorize $20 billion over 5 years for the Clean Water Act's program that assists municipal wastewater treatment projects (H.R. 3930, S. 1961). Neither bill received further action due to controversies about allocation of funds among the states and application of prevailing wage requirements in the Davis-Bacon Act.

Since the September 11, 2001 terrorist attacks in the United States, congressional attention has focused on security, preparedness, and emergency response issues, including at the nation's water infrastructure facilities (both wastewater and drinking water). In the 108th Congress, a bill authorizing grants to enhance security of wastewater treatment works has been approved by a House committee (H.R. 866).

BACKGROUND AND ANALYSIS
INTRODUCTION

The principal law that deals with polluting activity in the nation's streams, lakes, estuaries, and coastal waters is the Federal Water Pollution Control Act (P.L. 92-500, enacted in 1972), commonly known as the Clean Water Act, or CWA (amended by P.L. 95-217 in 1977, P.L. 97-117 in 1981, and P.L. 100-4 in 1987). It consists of two major parts: regulatory provisions that impose progressively more stringent requirements on industries and cities to abate pollution and meet the statutory goal of zero discharge of pollutants; and provisions that authorize federal financial assistance for municipal wastewater treatment plant construction. Both parts are supported by research activities, plus permit and enforcement provisions. Programs at the federal level are administered by the Environmental Protection Agency (EPA); state and local governments have major responsibilities to implement CWA programs through standard-setting, permitting, and enforcement.

The objective declared in the 1972 Act is to restore and maintain the chemical, physical, and biological integrity of the nation's waters. That objective was accompanied by statutory goals to eliminate the discharge of pollutants into navigable waters by 1985 and to attain, wherever possible, waters deemed "fishable and swimmable" by 1983. While those goals have not been fully achieved, considerable progress has been made, especially in controlling conventional pollutants (suspended solids, bacteria, and oxygen-consuming materials) discharged by industries and municipal sewage treatment plants.

Progress has been mixed in controlling discharges of toxic pollutants (heavy metals, inorganic and organic chemicals), which are more numerous and can harm human health and the environment even when present in minute amounts — at the parts-per-billion level. Moreover, efforts to control pollution from diffuse sources, termed nonpoint source pollution (rainfall runoff from urban, suburban, and agricultural areas, for example) are more recent, following the traditional focus on point source pollution (discharges from industrial and municipal wastewater treatment plants). Overall, data reported by EPA and states indicate that 39% of river and stream miles assessed by states and 45% of assessed lake acres do not meet applicable water quality standards and are impaired for one or more desired uses. Forty-four states now have some form of partial or statewide fish-consumption advisory in effect (including 100% of Great Lakes waters and a large portion of the nation's coastal waters), due to chemical contaminants in lakes, rivers, and coastal waters, and one-third of shellfishing beds are closed or restricted, due to toxic pollutant contamination.

The most recent major amendments were enacted in 1987 (P.L. 100-4); this was the first comprehensive revision to the law in a decade. Authorizations for a number of the provisions authorized in that law expired in FY1990 and FY1991, for programs such as general grant assistance to states, research, and general EPA support. Authorizations for wastewater treatment funding expired in FY1994. None of these programs has lapsed, however, as Congress has continued to appropriate funds to implement the Act.

The Clean Water Act has been viewed as one of the most successful environmental laws in terms of achieving its statutory goals, which have been widely supported by the public, but lately some have questioned whether additional actions to achieve further benefits are worth the costs. Such criticisms have come especially from industry, which has been the longstanding focus of the Act's regulatory programs and often opposes imposition of new stringent and costly requirements. Criticism also has come from developers and property rights groups who contend that federal regulations (particularly the Act's wetlands permit program) are a costly intrusion on private land-use decisions. States and cities have traditionally supported water quality programs and federal funding to assist them in carrying out the law, but recently many have opposed CWA measures that they fear might impose new unfunded mandates. Many environmental groups believe that further fine-tuning to strengthen the Act is needed to maintain progress achieved to date and to address remaining water quality problems.

Legislative Activity Since P.L. 100-4

Following enactment of amendments in 1987, no major CWA legislative activity occurred until the 104th Congress (1995). The House approved a comprehensive reauthorization bill, H.R. 961, that was opposed by environmentalists and the Clinton Administration which they said would undermine the existing framework for protecting U.S. waters. The Senate did not take up H.R. 961 or other CWA legislation.

In the 105th and 106th Congresses, no comprehensive reauthorization legislation was introduced, but action was taken in the 106th Congress on bills dealing with specific water quality issues. Congress passed a bill to strengthen protection of coastal recreation waters through upgraded water quality standards and coastal waters monitoring programs (P.L. 106- 284). Congress also passed a bill (P.L. 106-457) which reauthorized several existing CWA programs (i.e., Chesapeake Bay cleanup, clean lakes, and the National Estuary Program). Congress passed a bill to authorize CWA grant funding for wet weather sewerage projects (included as a provision of the FY2001 Consolidated Appropriations bill, P.L. 106-554).

During its tenure, the Clinton Administration did not offer proposals to reauthorize the CWA, but rather initiated a number of agency-wide and program-specific reforms focusing on flexibility and "common sense" approaches to regulation, many of which affected implementation of water quality programs. One initiative was a 1998 multi-agency Clean Water Action Plan intended to build on the environmental successes of the Act and address many of the nation's remaining water quality challenges. Besides EPA, other involved agencies were the Departments of Agriculture, Commerce, Interior, and the U.S. Army Corps of Engineers. The Bush Administration has not undertaken actions specific to the Clean Water Action Plan. Many of the Plan's activities continue, but without the focus given during the Clinton Administration.

107th Congress

The 107th Congress focused legislative attention on one of the key programs of the Act, provisions concerning financial assistance for municipal wastewater treatment projects. House and Senate committees approved bills to extend the Act's State Revolving Fund (SRF) program through FY2007 (H.R. 3930, S. 1961), but this legislation did not reach the floor in either chamber. Neither bill received further action, in large part due to controversies over application of prevailing wage requirements of the Davis-Bacon Act and over the formula for allocating SRF grants among the states.

The single water quality measure enacted by the 107th Congress was the Great Lakes Legacy Act (P.L. 107-303). It amends existing Great Lakes provisions of the CWA (Section 118) to authorize $50 million annually for FY2004-FY2008 for EPA to carry out projects to remediate sediment contamination in the Great Lakes. The bill also revises and reauthorizes CWA provisions concerning the Lake Champlain Basin Program. Miscellaneous provisions revive a number of CWA reports to Congress that had been sunset under a previously-passed law (P.L. 104-66) and allow states to use CWA Section 319 grant funds for stormwater management projects in FY2003.

More generally, following the September 11, 2001 terrorist attacks in the United States, congressional attention focused on security, preparedness, and emergency response issues. Among the topics of interest was protection of the nation's water infrastructure facilities (both drinking water and wastewater) from possible physical damage, biological/chemical attacks, and cyber disruption. Policymakers examined a number of legislative options in this area, including enhanced physical security, communication and coordination, and research. In October 2002, the House passed legislation to authorize $200 million in grants for security activities at wastewater treatment plants (H.R. 5169). It also authorized $15 million in technical assistance for small treatment plant facilities and $5 million to EPA for improved vulnerability assessment tools. Similar legislation was introduced in the Senate (S. 3037), but no further action occurred. Congress did enact legislation authorizing $160 million in grants for drinking water utilities to conduct vulnerability assessments (P.L. 107-188). In the 108th Congress, legislation similar to H.R. 5169 has been introduced and was approved by the House Transportation Committee on February 26 (H.R. 866).

ISSUES IN THE 108TH CONGRESS

The year 2002 marked the 30th anniversary of passage of the Clean Water Act and 15 years since the last major amendments to the law. While there has been measurable clean water progress as a result of the Act, observers and analysts agree that significant water pollution problems remain. However, there is less agreement about what solutions are needed and whether new legislation is required. Several key water quality issues exist: evaluating actions to implement existing provisions of the law, assessing whether additional steps are necessary to achieve overall goals of the Act which have not yet been attained, and defining the appropriate federal role in guiding and paying for clean water infrastructure and other activities. Legislative prospects for comprehensively amending the Act have for some time stalled over whether and exactly how to change the law. Many issues that might be addressed involve making difficult tradeoffs between impacts on different sectors of the economy, taking action when there is technical or scientific uncertainty, and allocating governmental responsibilities for implementing the law.

These issues partly explain why Congress has recently favored focusing legislative attention on narrow bills to extend or modify selected CWA programs, rather than taking up comprehensive proposals. Other factors also are at work. These include: a general reluctance by most Members of Congress to address controversial environmental issues in view of the slim majorities held by political parties in the House and the Senate; lack of presidential initiatives on clean water issues (neither the Clinton nor the Bush Administration has proposed CWA legislation); and since the terrorist attacks of September 11, 2001, a more prominent congressional focus on security and terrorism issues than on most other topics, including environmental protection.

Early indications from congressional leaders suggest that the 108th Congress, like the 107th Congress, will focus on water infrastructure funding legislation (see below). However, it is expected that the key authorizing committees (House Transportation and Infrastructure and Senate Environment and Public Works) will address other legislative priorities such as reauthorization of surface transportation funding and water resources development programs, before considering Clean Water Act legislation.

Water Infrastructure Funding

The Act's program of financial aid for municipal wastewater treatment plant construction is a central feature of the law. At issue today is how the federal government will assist states and cities, especially in view of the high projected funding needs that exist. Since 1972, Congress has provided $75 billion to assist cities in constructing projects to achieve the Act's requirements for secondary treatment of municipal sewage (equivalent to 85% reduction of wastes), or more stringent treatment where required by local water quality conditions. The CWA does not authorize funds for operation or maintenance of completed projects. State and local governments have spent more than $25 billion of their own funds for construction, as well. In addition to CWA programs, other sources of federal funding are administered by the U.S. Department of Agriculture and Department of Housing and Urban Development.

Nevertheless, funding needs remain very high: an additional $139.5 billion nationwide by 2016 for all types of projects eligible for funding under the Act, according to the most recent estimate by EPA and the states, completed in 1996. In September 2002, EPA released a study, called the Gap Analysis, which assesses the difference between current spending for wastewater infrastructure and total funding needs (both capital and operation and maintenance). EPA estimates that, over the next two decades, the United States needs to spend nearly $390 billion to replace existing wastewater infrastructure systems and to build new ones. Funding needs for operation and maintenance, which are not currently eligible for federal aid, are an additional $148 billion, the Agency estimates. According to the study, if there is no increase in investment, there will be about a $6 billion gap between current annual capital expenditures for wastewater treatment ($13 billion annually) and projected spending needs. The study also estimates that, if wastewater spending increases by 3% annually, the gap would shrink by nearly 90% (to about $1 billion annually). In addition to the Gap Analysis, EPA and states are preparing a new wastewater needs survey, as required by the CWA, which will update the 1996 survey. Outside groups, including a coalition called the Water Infrastructure Network, have offered proposals which have attracted some congressional interest for a multi-billion dollar investment program in wastewater and drinking water infrastructure.

The 1987 amendments initiated a program of grants to capitalize State Water Pollution Control Revolving Funds (SRFs), or loan programs. This program in Title VI of the Act replaced the previous categorical grants program, under which the federal share was 55% of project costs and localities were not obligated to repay federal funds that they received. Under the revolving fund concept, monies used for construction will be repaid by borrowing communities to the states, to be recycled for future construction in other communities, thus providing an ongoing source of financing. States must provide a 20% match of the federal amount. The intent of the 1987 amendments was that federal contributions to SRFs would assist in making a transition to full state and local financing by FY1995. The essential tradeoff was that states would have greater flexibility to set priorities and administer funding in exchange for ending federal aid after FY1994.

All states have established the mechanisms to administer the new loan programs and have been receiving SRF capitalization funds under Title VI for several years. Some with prior experience using similar financing programs moved quickly, while others had difficulty in making a transition from the previous grants program to one that requires greater financial management expertise for all concerned. Moreover, many states have complained that the SRF program is unduly complicated by federal rules, even though Congress had intended that states were to have greater flexibility. Congressional oversight since 1987 has examined the progress towards reducing the backlog of wastewater treatment facilities needed to achieve the Act's water quality objectives, but newer estimates of future funding needs, discussed above, are drawing increased attention from Members of Congress and others.

Small communities and states with large rural populations have experienced the largest share of problems with the SRF program. Many small towns did not participate in the previous grants program and consequently are likely to require major projects to achieve compliance with the law. Yet these communities often lack an industrial tax base and thus face the prospect of very high per capita user fees, if their citizens are required to repay the full capital cost of sewage treatment projects.

While the initial intent was to phase out federal support for this program, Congress has continued to appropriate SRF capitalization grants to the states, providing an average of $1.35 billion annually in recent years. The SRF provisions have been less controversial than others in the Act, such as wetlands reform, because of apparent general agreement on the need to extend funding assistance (as reflected in continued appropriations). The CWA's SRF provisions also were a model for similar provisions added to the Safe Drinking Water Act (SDWA) in 1996 (P.L. 104-182). However, because remaining clean water funding needs are still so large, at issue is whether and how to extend SRF assistance to address those needs, how to allocate SRF funds among the states, and how to prioritize projects and funding. Bush Administration officials have said that infrastructure funding needs go beyond what the federal government can do on its own. Of particular concern is assisting small and economically disadvantaged communities that have had the most difficulty in adjusting from the Act's previous categorical grants program to SRF loans. Additionally, there is interest in adequacy of SRF or other funding specifically for projects dealing with problems of overflows from municipal combined and separate sewers which can release partially or untreated wastewaters that harm public health and the environment. And more recently, wastewater utilities have sought assistance to assess operational vulnerabilities and upgrade physical protection of their facilities against possible future terrorist attacks that could threaten water infrastructure systems.

As described above, committees in the 107th Congress considered but did not pass legislation to address infrastructure funding issues. Water infrastructure funding legislation is expected to be a priority in the 108th Congress. Two bills to reauthorize the Clean Water Act funding program have been introduced so far (H.R. 20, S. 170). In addition, bills to reauthorize funding for sewer overflow grants (CWA Section 221) have been introduced (H.R. 784, S. 567). And, as described above, the House Transportation and Infrastructure Committee has approved a bill authorizing assistance to enhance the security of wastewater treatment works (H.R. 866).

Other Clean Water Act Issues

Several other CWA issues could receive congressional attention, through oversight hearings and possibly in legislative proposals.

TMDLs and State Water Quality Standards

The CWA requires states to identify pollution-impaired water segments and develop "total maximum daily loads" (TMDLs) that set the maximum amount of pollution that a water body can receive without violating water quality standards. A TMDL is essentially a budget to allocate responsibility for implementing pollution control measures within an area or watershed in order to remedy water quality impairments. Until recently, there had been little implementation of the TMDL provision (Section 303(d)), which Congress enacted in 1972. Since the early 1990s, environmental groups have filed lawsuits in 40 states to pressure EPA and states to meet the law's requirements. Of the suits tried or settled to date, 20 have resulted in court orders requiring expeditious development of TMDLs, thus driving the program that had previously received little attention. At issue today are controversies over implementation of the existing TMDL program and regulatory revisions that EPA issued in July 2000 partly in response to the lawsuits to strengthen the program. That rule has been highly controversial because of issues such as potential burdens on states, industries, cities and others to implement a revised TMDL program and potential impacts on some agriculture and forestry sources, which are not now directly subject to CWA regulations. The controversies also drew congressional attention, and 13 congressional hearings were held by the House and Senate committees during the 106th Congress. Committees and many Members expressed concern about details of the TMDL requirements and deadlines and adequacy of resources for states to develop TMDLs and related assessments. Because of those controversies, the Clinton Administration delayed the effective date of the 2000 rule until October 2001. In the FY2001 appropriations act providing funds for EPA, P.L. 106-377, Congress requested a study by the National Academy of Sciences (NAS) on the scientific basis of the TMDL program.

The NAS report, examining the role of science in the TMDL program, was issued June 15, 2001 (National Research Council, NAS, *Assessing the TMDL Approach to Water Quality Management*). It did not specifically analyze the July 2000 revised regulations. The NAS panel concluded that scientific knowledge exists to move forward with the TMDL program and recommended that EPA and states use adaptive implementation for TMDL development. In many cases, the report said, water quality problems and solutions are obvious and should proceed without complex analysis. In other cases, solutions are more complex and require a different level of understanding and something like phased implementation. In addition, the General Accounting Office issued a report which concluded that inconsistent monitoring, data collection, and listing procedures used by states to identify impaired waters have hindered efforts to develop effective TMDL programs (*Water Quality: Inconsistent State Approaches Complicate Nation's Efforts to Identify Its Most Polluted Waters*, GAO-02-186).

In October 2001, when the expected effective date of the 2000 rule was approaching, the Bush Administration announced that it would delay the rule for 18 months (until May 2003) to allow EPA officials time to review the rule and the NAS report. This action came after a federal court approved the Administration's request for a similar suspension of litigation which is challenging the regulation (nearly a dozen interest groups have sued EPA over various parts of the TMDL rule). In the interim, existing rules and requirements and court-sanctioned TMDL schedules (affecting approximately 20 states) remain in place.

On December 20, 2002, EPA proposed to withdraw the July 2000 TMDL rule while it considers initiating an entirely new rule or other options; no further timeframe was announced. EPA officials said that implementation of the existing TMDL program will continue in the meantime, but that additional time beyond May 2003 is needed to decide whether and how to revise the current program.

Congressional attention to these issues in the 107th Congress was limited to oversight hearings held by the House Transportation and Infrastructure Subcommittee on Water Resources in June and November 2001. The 108th Congress may examine implementation of existing TMDL requirements and possible regulatory changes, in view of continuing disagreement among states, cities, industry, and environmental advocates about program effectiveness and efficiency.

Regulatory Protection of Wetlands

How best to protect the nation's remaining wetlands and regulate activities taking place in wetlands has become one of the most contentious environmental policy issues, especially in the context of the CWA, which contains a key wetlands regulatory tool, the permit program in Section 404. It requires landowners or developers to obtain permits for disposal of dredged or fill material that is generated by construction or similar activity into navigable waters of the United States, including wetlands. Section 404 has evolved through judicial interpretation and regulatory change to become one of the principal federal tools used to protect wetlands, although that term appears only once in Section 404 itself and is not defined there. At the same time, its implementation has come to be seen as intrusive and burdensome to those whose activities it regulates. At issue today is how to address criticism of the Section 404 regulatory program while achieving desired goals of wetlands protection.

Unlike the rest of the Act, the permit aspects of Section 404 are administered by the U.S. Army Corps of Engineers, using EPA environmental guidance. Other federal agencies including the U.S. Fish and Wildlife Service (FWS) and Natural Resource Conservation Service (NRCS) have more limited roles in the Corps' permitting decisions. Tension has existed for many years between the regulation of activities in wetlands under Section 404 and related laws, on the one hand, and the desire of landowners to develop property that may include wetlands, on the other hand. The conflicts over wetlands regulation have for the most part occurred in administrative proceedings, as Congress has not amended Section 404 since 1977, when it provided exemptions for categories of routine activities, such as normal farming and forestry. Controversy has grown over the extent of federal jurisdiction and impacts on private property, burdens and delay of permit procedures, and roles of federal agencies and states in issuing permits.

Recent legislative proposals to modify Section 404 have presented a number of issues, including whether all wetlands should be treated the same, or whether some could be accorded less stringent regulatory protection; whether activities or areas covered by federal regulation should be modified; and whether federal and state roles in implementing Section 404 should be revised. Views on these issues vary. Many wetland protection advocates contend that statutory changes that have been proposed would weaken current protection efforts and that more modest administrative reforms would effectively improve the current program. Many landowners say that changes are needed to lessen burdens of the regulatory program. Some also argue that the CWA should compensate landowners whose property is adversely affected by regulatory "takings" when application of Section 404 limits desired property use, since an estimated 74% of all remaining wetlands are on private lands.

Proposals for comprehensive reform of wetlands regulatory programs have been controversial, leading some to focus instead on narrower revisions. Specific issues that could draw congressional attention include a 1998 federal court ruling that overturned a regulation (called the Tulloch rule) issued by the Corps and EPA in 1993 that had expanded the scope of wetlands regulation to certain landclearing and excavation activities that previously had not been regulated. The Clinton Administration issued a revised Tulloch rule before leaving office in January 2001, and after reviewing it, the Bush Administration agreed to let the rule take effect. The revisions were intended to clarify what types of landclearing and excavation activities are subject to regulation, in light of the 1998 court ruling. Industry groups have challenged the regulation in court.

Controversy also surrounds revised regulations issued by EPA and the Corps in May 2002 which redefine two key terms in the Section 404 program, "fill material" and "discharge of fill material." Under the regulatory program, the determination of what is "fill material" is important, since fill material is subject to Section 404 permit requirements of the Corps, while discharge of non-fill material is regulated by EPA under other CWA provisions. The agencies say that the revisions are intended to clarify certain confusion in their joint administration of the 404 program, but environmental groups contend that the changes allow for inadequate regulation of certain disposal activities, including disposal of coal mining waste. The Senate Environment and Public Works Committee held a hearing in June 2002 to review these issues. Legislation to reverse the agencies' action was introduced in the 107th Congress (H.R. 4683), but no further action occurred. Similar legislation has been introduced in the 108th Congress (H.R. 738).

The Supreme Court's SWANCC Decision

One issue involving long-standing controversy and litigation is whether isolated waters are properly within the jurisdiction of Section 404. Isolated waters that are wetlands which are not physically adjacent to navigable surface waters often appear to provide only some of the values for which wetlands are protected, such as flood control or water purification, even if they meet the technical definition of a wetland. On January 9, 2001, the Supreme Court ruled on the question of whether the CWA provides the Corps and EPA with authority over isolated waters. The Court's 5-4 ruling in *Solid Waste Agency of Northern Cook County (SWANCC) v. U.S. Army Corps of Engineers* (531 U.S. 159 (2001)) held that the Corps' denial of a 404 permit for a disposal site on isolated wetlands solely on the basis that migratory birds use the site exceeds the authority provided in the Act.

The full extent of retraction of the regulatory program resulting from this decision remains unclear for now. Environmentalists believe that the Court misinterpreted congressional intent on the matter, while industry and landowner groups welcomed the ruling. Policy implications of how much the decision restricts federal regulation depend on how broadly or narrowly the opinion is applied. The government's current view on this key question came in EPA-Corps guidance issued on January 15, 2003. It provides a legal interpretation essentially based on a narrow reading of the Court's decision, thus allowing federal regulation of some isolated waters to continue. Administration press releases say that the guidance demonstrates the government's commitment to "no-net-loss" wetlands policy. However, it is apparent that the issues remain under discussion within the Administration and elsewhere, because at the same time, the Administration issued an advance notice of proposed rulemaking seeking comment on how to define waters that are under jurisdiction of the regulatory program. Environmentalists oppose this effort, saying that the law and previous court rulings call for the broadest possible interpretation of the Clean Water Act. These groups are concerned that any such changes could result in narrowed regulatory protection of wetlands.

While it likely will take some time to assess how regulatory protection of wetlands will be affected as a result of the *SWANCC* decision and other possible changes, the remaining responsibility to protect affected wetlands falls on states and localities. Whether states will act to fill in the gap left by removal of some federal jurisdiction is unclear, but a few states (Wisconsin and Ohio, for example) have passed new laws or adopted regulations to do so. Legislation to overturn the *SWANCC* decision by providing a broad definition of "waters of the United States" was introduced in the 107th Congress (S. 2780, H.R. 5194), but no further action occurred. Similar legislation has been introduced in the 108th Congress (H.R. 962, S. 473).

In September 2002, the House Government Reform Subcommittee on Energy Policy, Natural Resources and Regulatory Affairs held a hearing on the government's response to the *SWANCC* decision and to press the government to clarify its interpretation of the Court case. Committee Members and public witnesses indicated that a lack of guidance has led to inconsistent regulatory decisions by Corps officials in individual regions of the country, and subsequent judicial decisions by other federal and state court have been mixed. At the hearing, Corps and EPA officials testified on their efforts to develop guidance, which subsequently was released in January.

Animal Waste Management: Regulating CAFOs

Public and policy attention has been increasing on steps to minimize public health and environmental impacts of runoff from animal feeding operations (AFOs). AFOs are agricultural facilities that confine livestock feeding activities, thus concentrating animal populations and waste. Animal waste is frequently applied to land for disposal and to utilize the nutrient value of manure to benefit crops. If not managed properly, however, it can pose risks to water quality and public health, contributing pollutants such as nutrients, sediment, pathogens, and ammonia to the environment. Existing EPA rules require large AFOs, termed Confined Animal Feeding Operations (CAFOs), to have CWA discharge permits, but EPA acknowledges that compliance with these rules has been limited. In 1999, EPA and the U.S. Department of Agriculture initiated a national AFO strategy to improve compliance and strengthen existing regulations that are intended to control adverse environmental impacts of these agricultural activities.

As part of that strategy (and to comply with a settlement agreement to update a number of industry clean water standards), in December 2000, EPA proposed rules to increase the number of CAFOs required to obtain CWA wastewater discharge permits and to restrict land application of animal wastes, in order to prevent runoff into nearby rivers and streams. The House Transportation and Infrastructure Water Resources subcommittee held an oversight hearing in May 2001 on this proposal, which would revise the existing regulations that have not been modified since they were issued in the 1970s. The hearing focused on impacts and costs of the proposal on the agricultural sector (especially small farms), which for the most part is not directly regulated by the Clean Water Act or other EPA programs.

EPA issued final revised CAFO rules on December 16, 2002. The final rules, which were published in the Federal Register on February 12 and are effective April 14, are generally regarded as less stringent than the December 2000 proposal. The most significant new provision will require CAFOs to develop nutrient management plans that are intended to keep livestock waste from entering nearby waters. Farmers are pleased that the rule scales back some of the proposal, which would, for example, have required co-permitting of corporate owners of livestock as well as of farmers who actually raise the animals. Environmentalists, however, contend the rule relies too heavily on voluntary measures to control runoff, instead of mandating strict compliance with water quality standards. A recent General Accounting Office report found that neither EPA nor states are equipped to implement the program, having not made provisions for additional staffing to process permits, conduct required inspections, and take enforcement actions (*Livestock Agriculture: Increased EPA Oversight Will Improve Environmental Program for Concentrated Animal Feeding Operations*, GAO-03-285). Several lawsuits challenging the final rules have been filed by industry groups and environmentalists. The 108th Congress may examine details of the final rules and overall efforts to address animal waste management problems.

CONGRESSIONAL HEARINGS, REPORTS, AND DOCUMENTS

U.S. Congress. House. Committee on Transportation and Infrastructure. Subcommittee on Water Resources and Environment. *Improving Water Quality: States' Perspectives on the Federal Water Pollution Control Act.* Hearing, Feb. 28, 2001. 107th Congress, 1st session, 53 p. (107-3)

—— *Water Infrastructure Needs.* Hearing, Mar. 28, 2001. 107th Congress, 1st session, 296 p. (107-8)

—— *Confined Animal Feeding Operations.* Hearing, May 16, 2001. 107th Congress, 1st session, 126 p. (107-21)

—— *The Wetlands Permitting Process: Is It Working Fairly?* Hearing, Oct. 3, 2001. 107th Congress, 1st session, 99 p. (107-50)

U.S. Congress. Senate. Committee on Environment and Public Works. *Water Investment* Act of 2002. Report to accompany S. 1961, together with minority views. 107th Congress, 2d session. Report 107-228. 116 p.

—— Subcommittee on Fisheries, Wildlife, and Water. *Water and Wastewater Infrastructure Needs.* Hearing, Mar. 21, 2001. 107th Congress, 1st session, 141 p. (S.Hrg. 107-316)

FOR ADDITIONAL READING

Houck, Oliver A. "TMDLs: The Resurrection of Water Quality Standards-Based Regulation Under the Clean Water Act." *Environmental Law Reporter News & Analysis*, v. 27, no. 7, July 1997: 10329-10344.

Loeb, Penny. "Very Troubled Waters." *U.S. News & World Report*, v. 125, no. 12, September 28, 1998: 39, 41-42.

National Research Council, National Academy of Sciences. ASSESSING THE TMDL APPROACH TO WATER QUALITY MANAGEMENT. National Academy Press, Washington, D.C. June 2001. 82 p.

U.S. Congressional Budget Office. *Future Investment in Drinking Water and Wastewater Infrastructure.* Washington, November 2002. 58 p.

U.S. Environmental Protection Agency. *The National Water Quality Inventory: 2000 Report.* Washington, September 2002. "EPA-841-R-2-001."

U.S. General Accounting Office. *Key EPA and State Decisions Limited by Inconsistent and Incomplete Data.* (GAO/RCED-00-54) March 2000. 73 p.

—— Water Infrastructure: Information on Financing, Capital Planning, and Privatization. (GAO-02-764) August 2002. 79 p.

Chapter 8

WATER QUALITY INITIATIVES AND AGRICULTURE

INTRODUCTION

Congress most recently enacted amendments to the nation's water quality law, the Clean Water Act (CWA), in 1987. But national water quality policy has evolved in the intervening years, as a result of implementation of the 1987 amendments and, even more so, as a result of Administration initiatives intended to fulfill the requirements and meet the goals and objectives of the Act as a whole. One of the most visible of these initiatives is the Clean Water Action Plan (CWAP), announced by President Clinton and Vice President Gore in February 1998. Its purpose is to build on the environmental successes of the CWA since it was enacted in 1972 and to address the nation's remaining water quality challenges through more than 100 actions now being developed or implemented by agencies of the government together with state, local, public and private partners. Somewhat less headline-worthy but likely to have widespread impact is implementation of an existing provision of the CWA, called the Total Maximum Daily Load (TMDL) program, reinvigorated and driven by lawsuits and recently issued regulatory changes.

The Clean Water Act's traditional focus has been on controlling wastewater from manufacturing and other industrial facilities, termed "point sources," which are regulated through discharge permits. That statutory and regulatory focus on point source controls has enabled much progress towards the nation's water quality goals. Yet, as point source pollution has been controlled, uncontrolled discharges in the form of runoff from "nonpoint sources" have become proportionally a larger share of remaining water pollution problems. Nonpoint pollution occurs as surface erosion of soil by water and as surface runoff of rainfall or snowmelt from diffuse areas such as farm and ranch land, construction sites, and mining and timber operations. Except for large animal feeding operations, most agricultural activities are considered to be nonpoint sources, since they do not discharge wastes from clearly identifiable pipes, outfalls, or similar "point" conveyances. Nonpoint sources are not required to obtain CWA discharge permits. Consequently, agricultural and other nonpoint sources are not subject to the compliance and enforcement regime that applies to point sources.

How is agriculture now involved in current water quality discussions? Agriculture, which has largely been at the sidelines of national water quality policies and programs, especially regulatory policies, since much of its activities are not directly subject to the Clean Water Act, now finds its activities scrutinized in connection with several aspects of the recent water quality initiatives, which are discussed in this report. First, one of the key goals of the CWAP is more effective control of nonpoint source pollution, and because water quality data identify agriculture as a significant contributor to nonpoint pollution, a number of actions in the Plan focus on agriculture as a whole. Second, one of the first Clinton Administration actions to carry out the CWAP was a national strategy for addressing waste management by one segment of agriculture, animal feeding operations (AFOs). This strategy will affect an estimated 15,000 to 20,000 of the largest animal feeding operations through regulation, and it seeks to encourage all livestock producers with smaller operations to adopt improved waste management practices voluntarily. A third development, separate from the CWAP, is implementation of the existing TMDL provision of the CWA which concerns measures to improve the quality of waters that remain impaired even after application of traditional pollution controls. It affects nonpoint as well as point sources of pollution from agriculture and other sectors. Where agricultural sources are identified as contributing to these continuing water pollution problems, they may be required by states to take steps that will help correct impairments.

Agricultural and other nonpoint sources have become increasingly prominent in debates over water quality policy in part because these types of diffuse sources are believed to be the largest remaining water pollution problem affecting United States waters. To begin to address these problems, Congress added section 319 to the CWA in 1987, directing states to implement programs for managing nonpoint sources. Consequently, under federal law, agricultural sources could be subject to statedeveloped plans requiring operators to use management measures to limit pollutant runoff from their lands. There is anecdotal information that some state nonpoint pollution programs are addressing agricultural runoff in various ways, including technical and financial assistance.[1]

In light of the several federal water quality policy initiatives discussed in this report, questions arise concerning how, specifically, agriculture will be affected. The answer, it seems, is that it will be affected substantially but not systematically, in that the effects do not grow out of an integrated policy aimed specifically at agriculture. The Administration and the individual federal agencies involved in these activities have produced voluminous reports and other documents detailing the overall CWAP and separate actions, but none describes *holistically* or *comprehensively* how agriculture or any other sector of the economy will be impacted overall. Still, substantial effect seems likely by virtue of the greater scrutiny in general that is being given to agriculture's impact on water quality. Operators of large animal feeding operations are especially affected by the Administration's AFO waste management strategy. Remaining impacts, especially of the TMDL program, depend very much on site-specific considerations of water quality impairments (i.e., what are the sources contributing to impaired waters, what will be the most effective ways to manage those sources) and how states will respond to the requirements of implementing the TMDL provision of the law. Each of the three initiatives will affect agriculture.

- In the Clean Water Action Plan, several key actions address agriculture, federal lands, and forestry as part of the overall goal in the Plan to more effectively control nonpoint source pollution. Specific outcomes, requirements affecting agriculture, if any, and deadlines, if any, will be evident as the key actions are set in motion.

- Under the AFO strategy, all operators of animal feeding operations should develop and implement site-specific comprehensive nutrient management plans, while an estimated 15,000 to 20,000 operators of AFOs (large facilities, which are termed confined animal feeding operations, or CAFOs, and smaller ones contributing to water quality impairments) will be priorities for regulatory programs and enforcement.

- As states implement the TMDL program, where agricultural sources are identified as responsible for water quality impairments, agriculture may be required to adopt control actions (for those in agriculture which are

---

[1] U.S. Environmental Protection Agency. *Section 319 Success Stories: Volume II. Highlights of State and Tribal Nonpoint Source Programs*. EPA 841-R-97-001. October 1997. 213 p.

point sources) and/or management measures (for agricultural nonpoint sources) to help clean up waterways. Determinations of impairments and required actions will be sitespecific and variable. However, there is controversy over whether nonpoint sources are lawfully covered by the TMDL program. If only point sources are covered, impacts on agriculture would be considerably fewer.

This chapter consists of three major parts providing background on the three ongoing water quality initiatives: the Clean Water Action Plan, the Unified National AFO Strategy, and implementation of the TMDL provisions of the Clean Water Act. At the end of the report is a glossary of terms and a chronology of the key deadlines that can be identified in the initiatives.

Linkage and Coordination

Each of the three initiatives described in this report contains deadlines for actions to be taken by federal agencies, states, and others. Based on the public documents associated with each, there is relatively little apparent coordination that would help agriculture or other sectors assess the aggregate impacts of all of these developments.

In the introductory part of the Clean Water Action Plan (discussed in Part 1 of this report), the Administration describes national data on water quality impairments and ongoing state efforts to identify pollution-impaired waters, as background for "today's water quality challenges" which the Plan addresses. Regarding agriculture, in addition to actions in the Plan related to reducing pollution from AFOs (discussed in Part 2), several other key actions also described in Part 1 specifically address agriculture, while others address federal lands and forestry. None of these is specifically tied to the AFO strategy.

The AFO strategy is one key action under the Clean Water Action Plan and, consequently, has obvious links to the Plan. In the AFO strategy, the principal linkage between it and the current TMDL program of the Clean Water Act (see Part 3 of this report) is in the strategy's discussion concerning the role of state and tribal governments, which are responsible for using the TMDL process to identify pollutionimpaired waters. There is explicit linkage of the AFO strategy with the TMDL program in one area. Under the AFO strategy, where TMDL assessments identify the causes of water quality impairment as coming, for example, from animal manure or wastewater problems, those assessments may be the basis for identifying AFOs which should be priorities for inclusion in the strategy's regulatory program.[2] However, CWA regulations issued in July 2000 to revise the TMDL program are separate from activities under the Clean Water Action Plan, including the AFO Strategy, and contain no discussion of actions under the Plan.

PART 1: THE CLEAN WATER ACTION PLAN[3]

In October 1997, on the 25th anniversary of the Clean Water Act (CWA), Vice President Gore announced an initiative intended to build on the environmental successes of that Act and to address the nation's remaining water quality challenges. While much progress has been made in achieving the ambitious goals of the law to restore and maintain the chemical, physical and biological integrity of rivers, lakes, and coastal waters, problems persist. Based on the limited water quality monitoring that is done by states, it is estimated that about 40% of those waters do not meet applicable water quality standards. The types of remaining water quality problems, especially runoff from farms and ranches, city streets, and other diffuse sources, are more complex than is controlling pollution discharged from the end of pipes at factories and sewage treatment plants.

The Vice President directed the Environmental Protection Agency (EPA) and the U.S. Department of Agriculture (USDA) to coordinate the work of other federal agencies to develop an Action Plan within 120 days to improve and strengthen water pollution control efforts across the country.[4] It was to focus on three goals: enhanced protection from public health threats posed by water pollution, more effective control of polluted runoff, and promotion of water quality protection on a watershed basis. The Departments of Commerce and the Interior and the U.S. Army Corps of Engineers also have roles. The purpose of the Action Plan is to coordinate federal efforts to achieve the three goals. Over all, the Initiative seeks primarily to address the wide range of activities that cause nonpoint source pollution (polluted runoff), including agriculture, mining, urban development, and forestry. EPA and states believe polluted runoff causes more than one-half of remaining water quality problems. Agriculture is believed responsible for the largest portion of today's water quality impairments due to

---

[2] U.S. Department of Agriculture, U.S. Environmental Protection Agency. "Unified National Strategy for Animal Feeding Operations." Mar. 9, 1999: 19-20.

[3] For additional information, see CRS Report 98-150, *The Clean Water Action Plan: Background and Early Implementation*; and CRS Report 98-745, *Clean Water Action Plan: Budgetary Initiatives*.

[4] "Notice of Vice President Gore's Clean Water Initiatives." 62 *Federal Register* 60447- 60449, Nov. 7, 1997.

polluted runoff--70% of impaired rivers and streams and 49% of impaired lakes, according to EPA.

Elements of the Plan and Early Implementation

President Clinton and Vice President Gore released the Action Plan on February 19, 1998 (the text is available at [http://www.cleanwater.gov/]). The components of the plan, more than 100 actions, correspond to specific elements identified by the Vice President in October 1997. It consists mainly of existing programs, including some planned regulatory actions that agencies have had underway, now to be enhanced with increased funding or accelerated with performance-specific deadlines. Components of the Action Plan announced in February 1998 are built around four key tools to achieve clean water goals:

- "A Watershed Approach," using a collaborative effort by governments, the public, and the private sector to restore and sustain the health of watersheds.

- "Strong Federal and State Standards," to protect public health, prevent polluted runoff, and ensure accountability.

- "Natural Resource Stewardship," calling on federal natural resource and conservation agencies to apply resources and technical expertise to state and local watershed restoration and protection.

- "Informed Citizens and Officials," calling on federal agencies to improve the information available to the public about the health of watersheds and safety of beaches, drinking water, and fish.

Many of the specific elements of the Plan are intended to address nonpoint source contributions to water quality impairments nationwide. According to the Plan and EPA reports, polluted runoff is now the major source of water quality problems in the United States. EPA's 1998 National Water Quality Inventory, which is the most recent compilation of conditions, summarizes state and tribal surveys of water quality; it indicates that about 40% of surveyed U.S. waterbodies are impaired by pollution, with the leading source being polluted runoff. About 60% of impaired rivers and streams and 30% of impaired lakes are impaired by runoff or discharges from agriculture.[5] In 28 states that specifically assessed impacts of agricultural activities on rivers and streams, the leading categories of agricultural source impairments were nonirrigated crop production, irrigated crop production, and animal operations (feedlots and animal holding areas).[6]

These water quality data are limited, because they describe only conditions in waters assessed by states and tribes, but do not include all waterbodies. For the 1998 report, states surveyed 23% of river miles, 42% of lake acres, and 30% of estuaries, since most states do not assess all of their waters during the two-year reporting cycle required by the Clean Water Act. Therefore, the data should be used with caution. Nevertheless, EPA believes that the data point to a major, continuing water pollution problem coming from agricultural sources of all types--crop and pastureland, rangeland, and concentrated animal feeding operations.

Regarding agriculture, a prominent key action in the Plan is reducing pollution from animal feeding operations (see Part 2 of this report). In addition, the Plan includes several other key actions concerning agriculture, such as: USDA will implement existing conservation reserve and conservation enhancement programs; USDA will work with agricultural producers to encourage the use of marketing and promotion orders to assist them in meeting pollution prevention objectives; and USDA will study the feasibility of providing an insurance program to enable producers to offset risks of utilizing new technologies by managing fertilizers and pesticides to prevent pollution (*Clean Water Action Plan*, pp. 50-54).

The Plan contains other actions to enhance watershed management on federal lands, starting with developing by 1999 a unified policy to provide a framework to ensure that federal land and resource management activities demonstrate water quality stewardship. Related actions include substantially improving maintenance of forest roads and trails on federal lands; publication of new forest transportation regulations by the U.S. Forest Service in 1999; assessment by EPA of whether to revise CWA permit regulations relative to forest roads; implementation of an accelerated program to restore stream corridors; actions by federal land management agencies to implement forest health strategies; and improved management of public rangelands (*Clean Water Action Plan*, pp. 32-36)

---

[5] U.S. Environmental Protection Agency. *National Water Quality Inventory: 1998 Report to Congress.* June 2000. EPA841-R-00-001. 1 vol. Broadly speaking, "impairment" means that the waterbody fails to attain and maintain designated water quality standards.

[6] Ibid., p. 65.

Early Implementation of the Clean Water Action Plan

The President's FY1999 budget identified the Clean Water Action Plan as a high priority for environmental programs. It requested a total of $2.5 billion--a $609 million, or 33%, increase over 1998 base funding levels--for a multi-agency Clean Water and Watershed Restoration Initiative. By October 1998, Congress had passed FY1999 appropriations bills to fund the Plan. Over all, the enacted bills provided $2.0 billion-- less than 10% of the increased funds sought by the Administration. EPA received close to full funding for its requested Action Plan activities, but USDA received less than 4% of requested increases for its activities under the Plan. In the President's FY2000 budget, the Administration requested $450 million in increases ($2.45 billion total) for the Plan. Appropriations bills provided $2.17 billion--$128 million more than in FY1999, but $322 million less than was requested. For FY2001, the President's budget requested $2.76 billion for activities under the Plan, a 27% increase above the FY2000 enacted funding level.

Federal officials estimated in February 1998 that the ambitious agenda in the Plan would require 25 years for full implementation. They believe that the Plan will be implemented, even though appropriations have been less than requested. A lack of new resources will mean a 50- or 100-year implementation schedule, they now say. The Administration has issued two reports (in February 1999 and February 2000, the anniversary of the release of the Action Plan) describing accomplishments to date. Many of the accomplishments, however, are only first steps in processes that will be lengthy, especially in terms of impacting water quality improvements. Since many of the specific items in the Plan and half of the budgetary resources are focusing on partnerships with states, localities, and individuals, accomplishments depend greatly on actions taken by multiple stakeholders. Changes in water quality conditions may not be apparent for many years.

EPA Activities

Of the 100-plus actions in the Plan, many involve core clean water programs for which EPA is primarily responsible.

- A significant aspect of the Plan is a focus on watersheds as the basis of water quality problem identification and decision making. In June 1998, EPA released a Unified Watershed Assessment Framework to assist states, tribes and others with the process called for in the Plan of identifying watersheds that do not meet clean water and other natural resource goals and where prevention action is needed to sustain water quality and aquatic resources. In response, states submitted watershed assessment reports by October 1, 1998. Funding increases provided since FY1999 for clean water grants to states have focused on priority waters identified by these assessments.

- State water quality reports indicate that over-enrichment of waters by nutrients (nitrogen and phosphorus) is the biggest overall source of impairment of the nation's waters. EPA is to publish numeric water quality criteria (scientific information concerning harmful levels of a pollutant) for nutrients for three groups of waters (lakes and reservoirs, rivers and streams, and estuaries and coastal areas) by the end of 2000 and for wetlands by the end of 2001. In June 1998, EPA released a national strategy for developing criteria and standards for nutrients. States will use these criteria to develop nutrient provisions of enforceable state water quality standards.

Joint or Other Federal Agency Activities
Many actions in the Plan involve other federal agencies, either alone or jointly with EPA. A key purpose of the Plan is to coordinate the several federal agencies and their state partners that have water quality program responsibilities.

- Among the areas that involve agriculture, a key element of the Plan, minimizing public health and environmental impacts of runoff from animal feeding operations (AFOs) into rivers, lakes, and estuaries, was addressed when EPA and USDA issued a national AFO strategy in March 1999. The strategy itself is not a new regulation or substitute for existing regulations, nor does it impose binding requirements on federal agencies, states, tribes, localities, or the regulated community. It presents an overall approach and timetable for curbing pollution from livestock operations. However, many of the details — and, hence, many of the specific impacts on operators, states, and others — will only become clear with the issuance of guidance and regulatory changes in the coming months. (See discussion below.)

- The Conservation Reserve Enhancement Program (CREP) is a state-federal conservation partnership program targeted to address specific state and nationally significant water quality, soil erosion, and wildlife habitat issues related to agricultural use. As of October 2000, USDA has approved programs in 13 states and is considering nine other proposals.

- In October 2000, EPA, USDA, the Departments of Agriculture, Commerce, Defense, Energy and the Interior, the Tennessee Valley Authority, and the Army Corps of Engineers adopted a unified federal policy on watershed management. It is intended to provide a framework for a watershed approach to ensure that federal land and resource management activities meet the goals of the Clean Water Act on the 800 million acres of land managed by the federal agencies and ensure that the federal government serves as a model for water quality stewardship.

- The Plan encouraged a temporary moratorium on new road construction in America's national forests. In October 1999, President Clinton directed development of an environmental impact statement and regulations to permanently prohibit new roads in certain roadless areas on national forest land. Regulations were proposed in May 2000. The proposal has been praised by some, criticized by some for not being far-reaching, and criticized by others for being too restrictive. Final rules are expected to be issued by the end of the year.

Litigation Challenging the Clean Water Action Plan

In June 1999, the Wyoming Association of Conservation Districts, joined by more than 60 groups representing state conservation districts and agriculture industry, challenged the Clean Water Action Plan in a lawsuit filed in U.S. District Court in Colorado.[7] The lawsuit alleges that the Plan violates three federal laws: the National Environmental Policy Act (NEPA), by not requiring an environmental impact statement on the plan's cumulative impacts; the Administrative Procedure Act (APA), by not providing enough opportunity for public comment; and the Clean Water Act, by trying to regulate nonpoint source water pollution. The plaintiffs seek to block implementation of the CWAP pending full compliance with the three laws.

The litigation asserts that, because the CWAP is a "major federal action," it should have been subject to the public notice and comment and intergovernmental coordination processes under the APA and NEPA. In response, EPA has argued that the Plan itself is a strategy for actions that the government plans to take and, thus, does not fall under federal public input requirements. Any EPA regulatory actions resulting from the Plan will be subject to such requirements, EPA has said.

In October 1999, the federal government filed a motion to dismiss the case, citing lack of jurisdiction and lack of subject matter. A U.S. Magistrate, appointed

---

[7] *Wyoming Association of Conservation Districts v. Browner*, D.Colo., 99-S-1179, June 23, 1999.

to analyze issues presented in the case, recommended in October 2000 that the government's motion to dismiss be granted by the district court. The plaintiffs oppose the recommendation, and the case is continuing.

Senate Oversight Hearing on the CWAP

On May 13, 1999, the Senate Environment and Public Works Committee held an oversight hearing on the CWAP, the first such congressional involvement outside the appropriations process.[8] The Committee heard from Administration and public witnesses. EPA and USDA witnesses defended the Plan as "a comprehensive blueprint for restoring and protecting the Nation's water resources." Environmental group witnesses endorsed the Plan because, in their view, it focuses significant federal resources on polluted surface runoff. State witnesses were divided. One from Maryland supported the Plan, saying it reinforces strong ongoing water quality programs in that state. A witness from Wyoming, which has been in dispute with EPA over the state's water quality program, said the Plan has disrupted ongoing state activities.

Agriculture industry witnesses challenged the scientific basis of the Plan, especially EPA's contentions that nonpoint sources generally and agriculture specifically are the major sources of water quality impairment. These groups argue that, because existing water quality data are limited and are based on partial state assessments of surface waters, the premise of the Plan is flawed. Better data are needed before undertaking such a broad initiative, they said. Others said that requirements and deadlines of actions in the Plan are unrealistic, particularly the animal feeding operations strategy (see Part 2).

PART 2: ANIMAL FEEDING OPERATIONS
AND THE CLEAN WATER ACT[9]

As noted previously in this report, most agricultural activities are considered to be nonpoint sources and thus are exempt from CWA regulatory programs; this includes most animal feeding operations (AFOs, or feedlots), where livestock are confined, reared, and fed. However, *large* confined animal feeding operations

---

[8] Other than this Senate oversight hearing, Congress has considered the CWAP primarily through the appropriations process, where spending decisions about requests to fund the Plan have been considered.

[9] For information, see CRS Report 98-451, *Animal Waste Management and the Environment: Background for Current Issues.*

(CAFOs) are specifically defined in the CWA as "point sources" rather than "nonpoint sources." CAFOs are treated in a similar manner to other industrial sources of pollution, such as factories and municipal sewage treatment plants, and are subject to the Act's prohibition against discharging pollutants into waters of the United States without a permit. In 1974 and 1976, EPA issued regulations defining the term CAFO for purposes of permit requirements (40 CFR §122.23) and effluent limitation guidelines specifying limits on pollutant discharges from feedlots (40 CFR Part 412). Discharge permits, issued by EPA or qualified states (43 states have been delegated this responsibility), implement the Part 412 requirements for individual facilities. Under the existing permit rules, a CAFO must meet all of the following criteria to be subject to EPA rules:

- Animals are stabled or confined and fed for 45 days or more in a 12-month period;

- Vegetation is not sustained during the normal growing season on any portion of the lot or facility (*i.e.*, animals are not maintained in a pasture or on rangeland);

- Feedlots hold more than 1,000 animal units[10] (or between 300 and 1,000 animal units if pollutants are discharged from a manmade conveyance or are discharged directly into waters passing over, across, or through the facility). Also, animal feeding operations that include fewer than 300 animal units may be designated as CAFOs if they pose a threat to water quality or use. Based on the USDA 1992 Census of Agriculture, EPA estimates that 6,600 feeding operations qualify as CAFOs, considering the number of animal units alone -- only 1.5% of the 450,000 operations nationwide that confine or concentrate animals.[11]

---

[10] As defined by USDA, an animal unit is 1,000 pounds of live weight of any given livestock species or combination of livestock species. This term varies according to animal type; one animal is not always equal to one animal unit. EPA's regulation of CAFOs covers AFOs consisting of: 1,000 beef cattle; 700 mature dairy cattle; 2,500 swine weighing over 55 pounds; 500 horses; 10,000 sheep; 55,000 turkeys; or 30,000 laying hens or broilers (with a liquid manure handling system).

[11] The concentration that has occurred in the animal agriculture sector is illustrated by changes over time in the number of CAFOs. When EPA's current CAFO regulations were proposed in 1975, USDA analyzed the potential impacts and reported that 95,000, or 13.6%, of the 700,000 animal feeding operations in the country would be subject to those rules. (Source: U.S. Department of Agriculture. "Implications of EPA Proposed Regulations of November 20, 1975 for the Animal Feeding Operations." Washington, DC, Jan. 30, 1976. 26 p.) The smaller number of total operations and smaller number of CAFOs today suggest that those that are regulated currently are, on average, much larger than 20 years ago.

EPA's effluent limitation regulations apply to operations that raise beef and dairy cattle, poultry, swine, sheep, and horses. The rules essentially prohibit discharge of wastewater from CAFOs into navigable waters, except when caused by the worst 24- hour storm that would occur in a 25-year period. These regulations do not specifically address discharges that may occur from wastewaters or solid manure mixtures which are applied to soil, nor do they address odor control or groundwater impacts from animal agriculture operations. These topics, if regulated at all, are subject to varied state and local authority, not federal law or regulation.

In addition to the CWA, the Coastal Zone Act Reauthorization Amendments of 1990 (CZARA) imposed waste management requirements on most livestock producers in the coastal zone of the 32 states and territories that participate in the Coastal Zone Management Act. CZARA is the first federal program to require specific measures to address agricultural erosion and runoff and other major sources of coastal nonpoint pollution. Its requirements are implemented by states through plans that they develop under CZARA. Federal CZARA guidance for agricultural sources specifies minimum management measures including retention ponds, solids separation basins, and vegetative practices such as filter strips between production facilities and nearby surface waters. CAFOs with as few as 50 animal units may be subject to these and other requirements. Federal agencies have fully approved CZARA programs in three states (California, Maryland, and Rhode Island) and conditionally approved CZARA programs in 26 other coastal states and territories (three others are under development). Livestock and poultry producers there will begin to be regulated by state requirements in the near future. Neither the law nor the implementing regulations specifies a timeline for implementation.

Problems with CAFO Regulation

A number of problems with the current CAFO regulatory system under the CWA have limited its effectiveness in preventing environmental problems from livestock production.

- Fewer than 30% of the CAFOs with over 1,000 animal units had or have CWA permits today (*i.e.*, about 2,000 out of 6,600). One explanation is the historic emphasis by federal and state regulators on other large industrial and municipal dischargers over agricultural sources, since most of agriculture is not subject to the Act. EPA estimated that only 760 permits were current at the end of 1995.[12] Another factor is disputes between regulators and agricultural operators over whether particular facilities meet the regulatory threshold, such as whether the regulations apply to feedlots that claim to have no discharge.

- Some sources went unregulated because the EPA rules, now more than 20 years old, do not reflect more recent changes in animal waste management technology. In particular, EPA defines feeding operations with 100,000 laying hens or broilers that use continuous flow watering systems and facilities with 30,000 laying hens or broilers that use liquid manure systems as CAFOs. However, the poultry industry has moved away from such wet systems since the 1970s. Many broiler producers now use dry litter waste systems where water is not applied and there is no discharge; they have argued that they are not subject to the rules. Producers of layers generally still have liquid waste systems.

- Federal regulations and guidelines contain no requirement for nutrient or manure management plans.

- CAFO inspections by federal and state regulators and compliance enforcement activities have been limited, often occurring only after citizen complaints or accidental releases following large rainfall events or equipment or facility failures.

Initiative under the CWAP: The National AFO Strategy

EPA has not lacked authority to address water quality problems associated with animal feeding operations, but doing so has not been a priority.[13] For several years, Agency officials discussed the need to revise the CAFO regulations, and in 1997, plans were announced for two initiatives -- one dealing with CWA enforcement against livestock producers, and one dealing comprehensively with all sources of nonpoint source pollution, including farm operations. However, neither included implementation details.

Several events combined to raise the priority of these topics. One was

---

[12] Parry, Roberta. "Agricultural phosphorus and water quality: a U.S. Environmental Protection Agency perspective." *Journal of Environmental Quality.* Vol. 27, no. 2 (1998): 258.
[13] CWA section 304(b) requires EPA to review and, if appropriate, revise effluent limitation guidelines at least annually. The CAFO standards have not been reviewed or revised since they were promulgated in the mid-1970s.

increasing attention to pollution incidents resulting from or believed to be associated with animal waste spills. Another was the growing number of lawsuits filed by environmentalists against states and EPA (involving nearly 2 dozen states), seeking to compel action against remaining sources of water pollution, including agriculture, under the Clean Water Act's TMDL program (see Part 3 of this report). A third came in February 1998 with the Administration's release of the Clean Water Action Plan.

The National AFO Strategy

In March 1999, EPA and USDA jointly issued a major program to implement the Clean Water Action Plan: a unified national strategy for animal feeding operations to minimize the water quality and public health impacts of AFOs.[14]

The strategy consists of multiple elements and is based on a national performance expectation that all AFO owners and operators—regardless of the size of their operations—will develop and implement by 2009 site-specific Comprehensive Nutrient Management Plans (CNMPs) intended to protect water quality and public health. Having all AFO owners and operators undertake comprehensive nutrient management planning will accomplish the goal of minimizing water pollution from confinement facilities and land application of manure, according to the strategy. With the exception of large AFO operations which are considered to be CAFOs and thus are subject to CWA requirements (about 5% of total AFOs nationwide), the agencies expect that the vast majority of CNMPs will be developed and implemented voluntarily. In general terms, a CNMP will identify actions or priorities to meet clearly identified nutrient management goals at an agricultural operation and typically will address manure handling and storage, land application of manure, land management (such as tillage, crop residue management, and other conservation practices), recordkeeping, and other utilization options (for example, when manure is sold to other farmers). Plans will be developed by qualified specialists. NRCS estimates that at least 330,000 AFOs need to develop CNMPs or revise existing nutrient management plans to meet the performance expectation of the strategy. The strategy recognized that technical and financial assistance will be needed both to develop and implement CNMPs, and it discussed additional resources in the Administration's budget to be directed at such assistance.[15]

---

[14] U.S. Department of Agriculture, U.S. Environmental Protection Agency. "Unified National Strategy for Animal Feeding Operations." Mar. 9, 1999. 46 p. Text of the strategy is available at [http://www.epa.gov/owm/afo.htm].

[15] The President's FY2001 budget requested an additional $151 million (for $325 million total) for the Environmental Quality Incentive Program (EQIP) and a $54 million increase (for $73

The strategy views regulatory programs as complementary to voluntary approaches that will apply to 95% of the total 450,000 AFOs in the nation. The strategy says that, under existing CWA authority, the discharge permit program in the CWA (called the NPDES program) will be used to address the relatively small number of AFOs (5% of the total) that cause measurable water quality or public health problems or that pose a significant risk to water quality or public health. It identifies the following priorities for permits and enforcement:

- Large facilities (those with greater than 1,000 animal units) which produce quantities of manure that can be a risk to water quality and public health. These already are considered to be CAFOs and therefore are "point sources" already subject to NDPES permit requirements.

- Some facilities with fewer than 1,000 animal units which can pose a risk of water pollution or public health problems, because the facilities have a manmade conveyance to discharge manure and wastewaters into streams.

- Other individual facilities or collections of facilities with fewer than 1,000 animal units that, based on water quality monitoring, are contributing significantly to impairment of a waterbody or watershed; such facilities will be designated as CAFOs and will be a priority for permit issuance and enforcement.

EPA expects that the total number of CAFOs meeting these three priorities for NPDES permits will be 15,000 - 20,000 facilities. These facilities will be required to develop and implement CNMPs, and their permits will include specific performance measures, monitoring, and reporting. Under the strategy, states and EPA should identify the universe of CAFOs and inspect all CAFOs in high-priority areas by 2001 and all other CAFOs by 2003. Permitting will occur in two phases. First, by 2005, EPA and authorized states will issue NPDES permits under existing regulations to priority facilities. EPA expects that this will occur mainly through general permits (either issued on a statewide basis or for specific geographic areas, such as watersheds). Individual permits will be issued to

---

million total) in USDA assistance to AFOs to develop or revise CNMPs. Appropriators (in P.L. 106-387) provided no increased funds for EQIP, but kept it at the FY1999 and FY2000 level of $174 million, and provided $33 million total for AFO assistance grants. The budget also requested an additional $50 million (for $250 million total) for the Section 319 nonpoint source management grant program, with the increase directed to priority watersheds under the Clean Water Action Plan. Appropriators (in P.L. 106-377) provided $238 million for that EPA grant program.

exceptionally large operations, new operations or those undergoing significant expansion, operations with historical compliance problems, or operations with significant environmental concerns. NPDES permits are issued for no longer than 5 years and must be renewed thereafter.

EPA also has initiated revisions to the existing CAFO permitting regulations and effluent guidelines, using input from USDA, states, tribes, other federal agencies, and the public. EPA currently is under a court-ordered schedule to issue revised guidelines for poultry, swine, and beef and dairy cattle by December 2002. In compliance with that schedule, EPA proposed revised guidelines for these sectors on December 15, 2000.[16] The proposed rule would increase the number of facilities required to obtain Clean Water Act permits and would restrict land application of wastes. In the proposal, EPA asked for public comment on two options for defining CAFOs subject to NPDES permitting. The first option would consider a facility to be a CAFO if it has 500 cattle or comparable animals units (compared with 1,000 animal units under current rules). The second option would define a facility as a CAFO if it has more than 1,000 animal units or has 300 to 1,000 animal units and meets certain conditions such as if they are located within 100 feet of a waterway. However, under either of the proposed options, permitting authorities would have discretion to designate smaller facilities (i.e., below 500 or 300 animal units, respectively) for inclusion in permit programs.

In other changes in the EPA December proposal, permitting requirements would be extended to dry-manure poultry operations and stand-alone immature swine and heifer operations. The Agency proposed to require that permitted facilities develop and implement site-specific permit nutrient plans which identify the amount of nutrients generated at the facility and determine rates for the application of the waste to agricultural land. EPA also proposed to lift the current regulatory exemption for facilities that only discharge during a 25-year, 24-hour storm.

Under the 1999 AFO strategy, in the second phase of NPDES permitting after 2005 (following expiration of permits issued between 2000 and 2005), EPA and states will reissue permits from the first round and will incorporate any new requirements that could result from regulatory revisions completed in the interim.

The AFO strategy also addressed corporate integrators, owners of livestock that contract out to farmers to raise the animals or poultry. It recommended a copermitting system, in which permits would cover not just the grower or farmer, but also the corporate owner, and EPA's December 2000 proposed CAFO rule changes would require co-permitting of facilities covered by those regulations. In

---

[16] For information, see: [http://www.epa.gov/owm/afos/rule.htm].

such a system, liability for handling the animal waste and for any environmental violations would be shared by the farmer and any corporate owner that exercises substantial operational control over a CAFO. Environmental groups in particular have urged copermitting, arguing that it could go a long way to improving waste management by involving integrators in ensuring that their contract growers are environmentally responsible. While some states already recognize that corporate owners share responsibility with farmers, industry groups have generally opposed this as a national requirement. In their view, it is inappropriate to hold the corporate entity responsible for an environmental violation when that entity does not own the farm, its buildings, the land, or the waste produced by the animals.

The strategy allows states that can show they meet the requirements of the NPDES program to be recognized by EPA as functionally equivalent. This part of the strategy recognizes that some states are implementing permitting programs under state law that meet or exceed the requirements of the NPDES program

Guidance on Permits

Both USDA and EPA have issued technical guidance documents intended to assist issuance of permits and development of comprehensive nutrient management plans. In May 1999, the Natural Resources Conservation Service of USDA released the Policy for Nutrient Management[17] and a revision to the conservation practice standards for Nutrient Management.[18] NRCS' policy directive and supporting technical guide establish policy for nutrient management, set forth guidance to NRCS personnel who provide nutrient management technical assistance, and guidance for the revision of the NRCS nutrient management conservation practice standard. These two documents will provide the framework for all nutrient management plans developed by NRCS for the agricultural community, which will be tailored by state conservationists within a two-year period.

In addition, in December 1999 NRCS released a draft document providing Technical Guidance for Developing Comprehensive Nutrient Management Plans.[19] Its purpose, USDA said, is not to establish regulatory requirements but to provide technical guidance for local, tribal, state, or federal programs to use in

---

[17] NRCS Policy for Nutrient Management, Part 402. Text of the policy is available at: [http://www. nhq.nrcs.usda.gov/BCS/nutri/gm-190.html]

[18] NRCS Nutrient Management (Code 590) Conservation Practice Standards. Text is available at: [http://www.nhq.nrcs.usda.gov/BCS/nutri/590.html]

[19] U.S. Department of Agriculture. Natural Resources Conservation Service. Notice of the Technical Guidance for Developing Comprehensive Nutrient Management Plans. 64 *Federal Register*, No. 236, Dec. 9, 1999: 68987-68994.

developing CNMPs. However, the document provides a list of six essential elements that need to be considered in developing a CNMP, including evaluation and treatment of sites proposed for land application, potential short- and long-term impacts of planning land application, feed management activities to reduce the nutrient content of manure, and consideration of alternative utilization strategies to land application (such as off-site transport, combustion to produce energy, or composting). NRCS expected to issue final Technical Guidance in July 2000 but has not done so yet.

In August 1999, EPA issued draft guidance and a model permit to assist the states in meeting the goal of accelerating issuance of NPDES permits for large CAFOs.[20] The guidance provides information on:

- Which facilities need to apply for an NPDES permit,

- The key elements of an NPDES permit for CAFOs,

- Components of a site-specific CNMP to be included in NPDES permits for CAFOs (the same six items specified in USDA's Technical Guidance document: manure and wastewater handling and storage; land application; site management; feed management; record keeping; and other utilization options, such as centralized treatment or composting),

- The relationship between NPDES permits and comprehensive nutrient management plans,

- The types of NPDES permits that may be issued to CAFOs (general permits issued on a statewide or watershed basis and individual permits, where appropriate),

- Public notice requirements,

- Co-permitting of corporate entities that exercise substantial operational control over CAFOs,

- Land application of manure and wastewater (including addressing land application activities under the control of the CAFO operator and activities not under the control of the CAFO operator), and

- Monitoring and reporting requirements.

---

[20] U.S. Environmental Protection Agency. Office of Wastewater Management. Guidance Manual and Example NPDES Permit for Concentrated Animal Feeding Operations. Review Draft. Aug. 6, 1999. 1 vol. [http://www.epa.gov/owm/afo.htm#Permit Guidance]

EPA anticipates that CAFOs will be required to develop and implement CNMPs that are consistent with EPA's permit guidance, other state requirements, and NRCS technical standards. EPA took public comment on the draft guidance through November 1999 and was expected to issue final guidance in March 2000. However, the guidance has not yet been issued.

Response to the Strategy

Strong reactions to the national strategy came from farm groups. A number of them expressed a fear that a national AFO strategy will enable EPA, through clean water rules, to control economic activity and land-use decisions of farmers.[21] Most would prefer that any animal waste program focus on voluntary approaches that encourage operators to utilize good environmental practices, with regulation and enforcement limited to only known problems of poor resource management. Agricultural groups criticized many parts of EPA's draft permit guidance to implement the strategy, contending, for example, that EPA lacks authority to require co-permitting.

From the states' perspective, many have questioned the need for a national program. A key concern for states has been that many already have difficulty providing resources for feedlot inspections and enforcement; thus, they are wary of new regulatory requirements that could impose additional resource burdens. States also say that they need flexibility to coordinate and prioritize implementation of the federal strategy with other equally important state programs. EPA's concern is to balance the states' desire for flexibility with the federal agency's desire to have state programs be accountable and provide an opportunity, if needed, for federal enforceability.

Environmentalists say that the proposed timeline to implement the strategy (7 years to issue permits for all CAFOs) is too slow. Many are critical that EPA failed to act on this problem sooner. Environmentalists often are skeptical of voluntary approaches to managing animal waste, particularly where there is no requirement for water quality monitoring or reporting, and little or no public involvement in siting, permitting, or similar decision making.[22] Environmental groups were highly critical of EPA's draft permit guidance. In their view, the guidance document inappropriately delegates responsibility to set nutrient waste management standards to USDA, which the Clean Water Act does not allow. According to these groups, comprehensive nutrient management plans based on

---

[21] "Farm Groups Fear Regulatory Intrusion." *Land Letter*, Jan. 28, 1999: 2.
[22] "Farmers, Environmentalists Blast EPA Plan to Control Polluted Runoff," *Inside E.P.A.*, Mar. 12, 1999: 13.

USDA standards will be inadequate and will not provide for compliance with the Clean Water Act.

Appropriations Requirement

In the conference report accompanying EPA's FY2000 appropriation (P.L. 106-74, H.Rept. 106-379), conferees directed EPA, in conjunction with USDA, to conduct a cost and capability assessment of the AFO strategy and ordered that the report be submitted to Congress by May 15, 2001.[23]

PART 3: RELATED WATER QUALITY INITIATIVE: TMDLS[24]

The Clean Water Act (CWA) contains a number of complex elements of overall water quality management. Foremost is the requirement in section 303 that states establish ambient water quality standards for surface waterbodies. These consist of the designated use or uses (e.g., recreational, public water supply, or industrial water supply) and the water quality criteria which are necessary to protect the use or uses. Through permits, states or the EPA impose wastewater discharge limits on individual industrial and municipal facilities to ensure that water quality standards are attained. However, Congress recognized in the Act that, in many cases, pollution controls implemented by industry and cities would be inadequate, due to pollutant contributions from other unregulated sources or insufficient regulation of cities and industrial facilities.

Under section 303(d) of the Act, states must identify lakes, rivers, and streams for which wastewater discharge limits are not stringent enough to achieve established water quality standards, after implementation of technology-based controls by industrial and municipal dischargers. For each of these waterbodies, a state is required to set a total maximum daily load (TMDL) of pollutants at a level that ensures that applicable water quality standards can be attained and maintained. If a state fails to do the TMDL analysis, EPA is required to develop a priority list for the state and make its own TMDL determination.

Section 303(d) provides the analytical and regulatory means for using water quality standards to upgrade waters that remain polluted after the application of technology-based requirements. A TMDL includes a quantitative assessment of water quality problems, pollution sources, and pollutant reductions needed to

---

[23] H.Rept. 106-379, in the *Congressional Record*, daily ed., October 13, 1999: H10019.
[24] For additional information, see CRS Report 97-831, *Clean Water Act and Total Maximum Daily Loads (TMDLs) of Pollutants*.

restore and protect a river, stream, or lake. TMDLs may address all pollution sources, including point sources such as municipal sewage or industrial plant discharges; nonpoint sources, such as runoff from roads, farm fields, and forests; and naturally occurring sources, such as runoff from undisturbed lands. The complexity and cost of developing TMDLs will vary, depending on the geographic area, number and complexity of pollutants, and distribution of sources.

The TMDL program first and foremost affects states, territories, and Indian tribes authorized to administer the Clean Water Act. It requires these entities to adopt and implement measures needed to attain and maintain water quality standards. It is up to states, territories, and tribes to identify waters that do not meet this goal and adopt policies and measures applicable to individual sources, as appropriate to attain water quality standards. In the early years of implementing clean water programs, states and localities were largely focused on water pollution problems associated with point sources (industries and municipalities). The TMDL requirements of the law effectively force an examination of *all* sources contributing to water quality problems. Thus, EPA, states, and the public are looking beyond traditional point source controls to assess all measures needed to attain water quality standards. This broader assessment is occurring as a result of litigation which has forced action by states and EPA and more recently by changes to the TMDL regulations.

A TMDL is not self-implementing and does not itself establish new regulatory controls on sources of pollution. However, when TMDLs are established, municipal and industrial wastewater treatment plants may be required to install new pollution control technology. States and EPA enforce the TMDLs through revisions to existing permits which include the pollutant limits and a schedule for compliance. For waters impaired by nonpoint source runoff, including runoff from agriculture, because there are no federal controls over these sources under the Clean Water Act, the primary implementation measures are state-run nonpoint source management programs coupled with state, local, and federal land management programs and authorities. For example, farmers and ranchers may be asked to use alternative methods in their operations to prevent fertilizers and pesticides from reaching rivers. Cities may be required to control and treat runoff from their streets.

Implementation

TMDLs are one element of water quality management programs conducted by states to implement the CWA. Other activities include standard setting, monitoring, issuing permits, and enforcement. Integrating them with the TMDL program may well be difficult because of factors such as different program purposes, schedules, and even different definitions for key terms. Most states have lacked the resources to do TMDL analyses, which involve complex assessment of all identified point and nonpoint sources to ascribe and quantify environmental effects for particular discharge sources. Baseline water quality monitoring data for the analyses (to identify impaired waters and pollution sources) is limited. EPA has both been reluctant to intervene in the states and has also lacked resources to do so itself. Thus, there has been little implementation of the provision which was enacted in 1972. For many years, EPA did little even to prod states to identify waters that remain pollution-impaired, much less undertake analyses to develop TMDLs, as required by the Act. The first TMDL regulations were issued in 1985, but only in 1992 did EPA issue regulations requiring states every 2 years to list waters that do not attain water quality standards and establish TMDLs to restore water quality. Under this schedule, states submitted their most recent 303(d) lists in April 1998. From these 1998 submissions, EPA estimates that approximately 20,000 waterways nationwide are impaired and require TMDLs.

Lawsuits have driven the greatest attention to TMDLs. Responding to the failure of both states and EPA to meet the statutory requirements, environmental groups have filed 40 lawsuits in 38 states in the last few years. The first such lawsuit was filed in 1986; the bulk have been filed since 1992. Environmentalists see implementation of section 303(d) as important both to achieving the overall goals and objectives of the Act and to pressuring EPA and states to address nonpoint and other sources which are responsible for many water quality impairments nationwide. Courts in a number of states have ordered or approved settlements for expeditious development of TMDLs.[25]

Because of the lawsuits and existing requirements of the law, in August 1997, EPA issued a policy which for the first time called on states to develop long-term schedules for implementing TMDLs. Under that policy, EPA directed states to establish TMDLs in order to meet water quality standards within 8 to 13 years.[26] One observer commented on this time frame, "Whether even this pace can be maintained, and whether it will produce load allocations and plans of sufficient

---

[25] For information on TMDL litigation by state, see EPA's Web site: [http://www.epa.gov/OWOW/tmdl/lawsuit1.html].

[26] This is a longer time frame than is being mandated as a result of some of the TMDL litigation. The schedules for TMDLs in 19 lawsuits concluded by consent decrees and settlement agreements range from 4-1/2 years to 12 years.

quality to be effective, are legitimate and difficult questions."[27] Following listing of impaired waters, pursuant to section 303(d), development of TMDLs is being initiated at an increasing pace in some states, but most TMDLs remain to be completed. EPA estimates that about 1,500 TMDLs have been developed. Evidence of cleanup of waterways will take much longer to identify.

Estimating when individual waters will actually be cleaned up, following development of a TMDL, is difficult. The amount of time required for a waterbody to reach water quality standards can vary considerably, depending upon the complexity of the pollutants, the uses of the land surrounding the waterbody, and the commitment of the community or upstream dischargers to reducing pollutants. EPA's current regulations do not contain cleanup deadlines or targets.

Proposed Regulatory Changes

In August 1999, EPA proposed comprehensive revisions to the TMDL regulations to strengthen the program.[28] The proposal set forth criteria for states, territories, and authorized Indian tribes to identify impaired waters and establish all TMDLs within 15 years. The proposal incorporated many of the recommendations of a Federal Advisory Committee Act (FACA) group which the Agency convened in 1996 to help develop a consistent national program.[29] At least two aspects of the proposal were controversial: (1) an explicit requirement that waterbodies impaired wholly or in part by nonpoint sources of pollutants be identified and that TMDLs be developed for such waters, and (2) a new requirement for an implementation plan. Further, explicit inclusion of nonpoint sources of pollution and potential impacts on agriculture and silviculture sources became highly contentious.[30] Vigorous challenge to all parts of the proposal came from states and various industry groups, arguing that EPA's proposed expansion of the current TMDL program is not clearly authorized in the law. EPA responded that it does have ample authority for the proposed changes.

Because of wide interest in the proposal, EPA extended the public comment period on the TMDL rule by 90 days, to Jan. 22, 2000, for a total comment period

---

[27] Houck, Oliver A. "TMDLs, Are We There Yet?: The Long Road Toward Water Quality-Based Regulation under the Clean Water Act." *Environmental Law Review*, v. 27, August 1997 p. 10399.

[28] 64 *Federal Register* No. 162, Aug. 23, 1999. pp. 46011-46055.

[29] U.S. Environmental Protection Agency. REPORT OF THE FEDERAL ADVISORY COMMITTEE ON THE TOTAL MAXIMUM DAILY LOAD (TMDL) PROGRAM. July 1998. 1 vol. Available at: [http://www.epa.gov/OWOW/tmdl/advisory.html#fdr].

[30] For additional information, see CRS Report RL30422, *EPA's Total Maximum Daily Load (TMDL) Program: Highlights of Proposed Changes and Impacts on Agriculture*.

of 150 days. The Agency received an estimated 34,000 comments.

EPA's 1999 proposal had few strong supporters, for varying reasons. States, which would be directly affected by the proposal, criticized the burdens that new requirements would place on them. They are concerned that they lack the resources to meet tight deadlines to develop and implement TMDLs. Further, states say that TMDLs should not necessarily be prioritized over other elements of existing water quality management programs. Industry groups are concerned about impacts of new pollution control requirements. But, municipal and industrial point source groups urge states and EPA to ensure that TMDL requirements do not fall disproportionately on their discharges, while possibly failing to address nonpoint source contributions to impaired waters. Farm groups and others associated with nonpoint discharges question EPA's authority to include nonpoint source pollution in the TMDL program. The forestry industry vigorously criticized the potential impacts of the proposal on its activities. A number of environmentalists, who support the need for a stronger TMDL program, objected to the lengthy time periods in the proposal before water quality improvements are likely to occur. They criticize the lack of aggressive implementation of a program that has existed in the law since 1972.

Congressional interest has been high: during the 106th Congress, 13 congressional hearings were held, and six legislative proposals to modify the Clean Water Act or delay the rule were introduced.[31] EPA attempted to respond to the widespread criticism and signal flexibility on some of the most contentious points. While the revised TMDL rule was undergoing final Administration review, Congress adopted a provision in H.R. 4425, the FY2001 Military Constructions/FY2000 Urgent Supplemental Appropriations Bill, stating that no funds may be used in FY2000 or FY2001 to "make a final determination on or implement any new rule relative to" the August 1999 TMDL proposal. Because the President intended to sign H.R. 4425 into law but opposed the TMDL provision, the Administration accelerated its review, allowing the EPA Administrator to sign it on July 11 before the appropriations bill was signed on July 13 (P.L. 106-246). In the final rule, EPA acknowledged Congress' action in H.R. 4425 and delayed the effective date of the rule's program changes until 30 days after October 1, 2001, or the expiration of the rider, whichever comes first.

---

[31] Since October 1999, hearings have been held by the full committee or subcommittees of the House Agriculture Committee, House Transportation and Infrastructure Committee, Senate Agriculture, Nutrition and Forestry Committee, and Senate Environment and Public Works Committee. Legislative proposals in the 106th Congress include H.R. 3609, H.R. 3625, H.R. 4502, S. 2041, S. 2139, and S. 2417. Another bill, H.R. 4922, was introduced after promulgation of the final rule in July.

In the interim, current program requirements under existing regulations and court-sanctioned TMDL schedules remain in place. The text of the final rule was published in the *Federal Register* on July 13.[32]

The Revised TMDL Regulation

Current law and the existing TMDL program require states to identify waterbodies where water quality standards are not being attained and to establish a total maximum daily load of pollutants at a level that will attain water quality standards by allocating further required pollutant reductions among sources. The key changes proposed in August 1999 included: a new requirement for a more comprehensive list of impaired and threatened waterbodies; a new requirement that states, territories and authorized Indian tribes establish and submit schedules for establishing TMDLs; a new requirement that the listing methodologies be more specific, subject to public review, and submitted to EPA; clarification that TMDLs include nine specific elements; a new requirement for an implementation plan as a required element of a TMDL; and new public participation requirements.

The July 2000 final rule comprehensively revises current TMDL regulations. It builds on the current regulatory program and adds details, specific requirements, and deadlines. It retains the basic elements of the 1999 proposal for more comprehensive identification of impaired waters, schedules and minimum elements for TMDLs, and new public participation requirements.[33] The final revised program rule establishes new requirements for listing impaired waters and requires schedules for completing TMDLs (the current program has no TMDL time schedules). It also establishes 11 minimum requirements for the content and development of TMDLs, including an implementation plan as a required element of a TMDL. Under the CWA, if a state fails to develop the list of impaired waters or develop a TMDL, EPA is required to do so. For states, the revised TMDL rules increase their responsibilities to identify impaired waters in four ways: revising the identification/listing methodology, establishing schedules for TMDL development, increasing public participation, and providing the identification/listing methodology in a new format.

For some interested parties, what is most of interest is what was **not** included

---

[32] U.S. Environmental Protection Agency. "Revisions to the Water Quality Planning and Management Regulation and Revisions to the National Pollutant Discharge Elimination System Program in Support of Revisions to the Water Quality Planning and Management Regulation; Final Rules." 65 *Federal Register* No. 135, July 13, 2000, pp. 43586-43670.

[33] For detailed information, see CRS Report RL30611, *EPA's Total Maximum Daily Load (TMDL) Program: Highlights of the Final Revised Rule.*

in the final rule. EPA dropped several provisions that were most controversial in the proposal, including some potentially affecting agriculture and forestry.

Agriculture and Forestry

The final rule entirely dropped provisions that could have affected some agricultural and forestry activities and could have required some of them to obtain CWA discharge permits if they are contributing to water quality impairments. Much of the criticism of the TMDL proposal had focused on possible impacts on these sources, most of which currently are exempt from the Act's permit and enforcement requirements that apply to point source discharges from industries and municipalities. These parts of the proposal, especially those potentially affecting forestry, generated vigorous criticism (and, according to EPA, more than one-half of the 34,000 public comments submitted on the TMDL proposal), and much of EPA's response since August 1999 focused on explaining and clarifying provisions that were, in fact, a small part of the full TMDL proposal.

In 1999, EPA proposed that some forestry operations, animal feeding operations (AFOs), and aquatic animal production facilities not currently subject to CWA permits could be required by states to obtain permits. EPA justified the proposal on the basis that state water quality data indicate that pollutants from agriculture and forestry are causing water quality problems that prevent waters throughout the nation from meeting standards. The proposal detailed a narrow set of circumstances when this might occur – for example, only where there is an identifiable source of discharge, only where the discharge is causing a water quality impairment, only where the source is determined to be a significant contributor of pollutants to the impaired waterbody, and only where EPA is developing the TMDL in lieu of a state. However, agriculture and forestry groups strongly criticized the possibility that even some part of their activities could be subjected to CWA regulations.

Concerns of the forestry industry included challenging whether forestry's water quality impacts are significant enough to warrant EPA's proposed changes, suspicion that the reach of EPA's program would be broader than the Agency indicated, and a general fear of becoming subject to CWA regulation and enforcement. Before finalizing the revised rules, EPA first indicated that the provisions affecting forestry would be withdrawn for reproposal at a later date. But in the final rule, the Agency indicated that the forestry, AFO, and aquatic animal facilities provisions were dropped and that EPA does not intend to repropose any of them.

Treatment of Nonpoint Sources in the TMDL Program

One of the most contentious TMDL issues has been whether discharges from agricultural and other nonpoint sources are included in the program or whether it is limited to point source impairments of waterbodies.

EPA points out that agency policy and rules since 1985 have fully included identification of waters impaired by all sources: point sources, nonpoint sources, and a combination of both. Further, administrative guidance documents on TMDL implementation likely have included all sources. Practically speaking, however, nonpoint sources have infrequently been affected by TMDL requirements, at least until recently, because of several factors: (1) limited state and federal implementation of section 303(d), especially before recent litigation and EPA's response to lawsuits, and (2) EPA's and states' long-standing focus on controlling pollution from point sources, which has changed in part as a result of data indicating that nonpoint pollution is a significant source of water quality impairments nationwide.

EPA's 1999 proposal and the final rule clarify that states are to identify waters impaired by all sources and to establish TMDLs whether the impairments are due to pollutants from point sources, nonpoint sources, or a blend of sources. In the proposal, EPA explained (64 *Federal Register* 46020-46021) its view that section 303(d) provides ample authority to list waterbodies impaired by nonpoint sources of pollution and to establish TMDLs for those waterbodies. In EPA's view, this is primarily because there is no express exclusion of nonpoint source-impaired waterbodies from the TMDL requirements of section 303(d) and because the definition of "pollutant" in the Act is not limited to point sources.

Some agriculture and forestry interests fear that, by including nonpoint source pollutants in TMDLs, EPA will *regulate* nonpoint sources pursuant to section 303(d) by requiring pollutant reductions from nonpoint sources. In response, EPA acknowledged in the July 2000 final rule that the Clean Water Act does not authorize the Agency to regulate nonpoint sources and that nonpoint source load reductions can only be required by states through their implementation of the Act. EPA's only ability to affect or encourage implementation of TMDLs involving nonpoint sources is indirect, by conditioning grants to states (e.g., CWA section 319 grants).[34]

Inclusion of nonpoint sources in the TMDL program remains a controversial topic.[35] However, groups representing major point source dischargers are

---

[34] 65 *Federal Register* 43632, July 13, 2000.

[35] In northern California, a group of farmers, plus agricultural and timber trade associations, challenged EPA's authority to control pollutant allocations to waters impaired solely by nonpoint sources. Plaintiffs in the lawsuit claimed that the CWA does not give EPA the

concerned that if arguments against including nonpoint sources are successful, point sources will be unfairly and inequitably targeted to achieve more stringent water quality controls.

If EPA's views that section 303(d) applies to nonpoint source pollutants are ultimately rejected by the courts or policymakers, impacts of the TMDL program on agriculture would be considerably less, and fewer agricultural sources would be affected by TMDL requirements. However, barring change in the current policy, agriculture and forestry sources are not sheltered from the substance of the TMDL program. As states continue to implement both the current program under existing rules and the revised program in the future, if agricultural and forestry nonpoint sources are identified as contributing to water quality impairments, states may seek controls or management practices by those sources in order to attain water quality standards. Under both the existing and revised TMDL program, states are responsible for identifying impaired waters and allocating pollutant reductions needed to attain water quality standards. The revised program adds details, specificity, and deadlines to the existing program, but in either case, where nonpoint sources are associated with water quality impairments, states may call for measures (voluntary or otherwise) that will achieve necessary pollutant load reductions.

Moreover, concerning animal feeding operations, other federal activities independent of the TMDL program – i.e., implementation of the EPA-USDA AFO Strategy discussed previously -- could lead to more stringent regulation of some.

Further Developments

Litigation challenging the July final TMDL rule has been filed in the federal District Court for the District of Columbia. Lawsuits have been filed by several industry and trade association groups representing nonpoint source dischargers. These suits argue, among other points, that EPA exceeded its authority in seeking to regulate agricultural and other nonpoint source operations. Two lawsuits have been filed by groups representing point source dischargers. Some in these groups raise legal issues about listing of impaired waters and similar implementation problems that could adversely affect utilities and other industries. Finally, several

---

authority to regulate nonpoint sources such as agricultural runoff. In March 2000, a federal district court rejected the plaintiffs' arguments and held that it would be impossible to carry out the TMDL program and implement water quality standards without taking nonpoint sources into

environmental groups have filed to intervene for the defense in some of the lawsuits and have also filed lawsuits of their own challenging parts of the final rule that they believe are not strong enough. The deadline for filing legal challenges was November 24, but EPA was reportedly seeking to extend that deadline through January 2001.

The FY2001 appropriation bill providing funds for EPA, P.L. 106-377, includes report language (H.Rept. 106-988) directing studies by the National Academy of Sciences on the scientific basis of the final TMDL rule and by EPA on the potential costs to states and businesses of implementing the revised TMDL rule. EPA also is to prepare a report on monitoring data needed to develop and implement TMDLs. The NAS report is to be submitted to Congress by June 1, 2001. The EPA report is to be submitted to Congress by February 21, 2001 (120 days after enactment of P.L. 106-377).

Under the Congressional Review Act, Congress has the opportunity to review an agency's rule and can disapprove the rule by passing a joint resolution, which the President could approve or disapprove, like any other bill presented for his signature. Joint resolutions to disapprove the TMDL rule were introduced in the House (H.J.Res. 104, H.J.Res. 105, and H.J.Res. 106) and in the Senate (S.J.Res. 50). Pursuant to the Congressional Review Act, Congress has 60 session or legislative days to pass a joint resolution of disapproval. Because the session or legislative days between introduction of these resolutions and the end of the 106th Congress was less than 60 days, the Act provides that a joint resolution of disapproval could be re-filed in the 107th Congress, and the new Congress would then have 45 days to conduct a review of the rule. If such a resolution passed both Houses of Congress and was signed by the President, the rejected rule would be deemed not to have had any effect at any time, and current TMDL regulations would remain in effect.

---

account (*Pronsolino v. Marcus*, 91 F.Supp.2d 1337 (N.D. Cal. 2000)). The case has been appealed.

GLOSSARY OF TERMS

Animal feeding operation (AFO): Agricultural enterprises where animals are kept and raised in confined situations. AFOs congregate animals, feed, manure and wastewater, and production operations on a small land area. Feed generally is brought to the animals, rather than the animals grazing or otherwise seeking feed in pastures, fields, or on rangeland.

Animal feeding operations strategy: A Plan issued jointly by USDA and EPA in March 1999 as part of the CWAP with the goal of having AFO owners and operators take actions to minimize water pollution from animal confinement facilities and land application of manure.

Animal unit (AU): As defined by USDA, an animal unit is 1,000 pounds of live weight of any given individual livestock species or combination of livestock species.

Clean Water Act (CWA): Federal Water Pollution Control Act (P.L. 92-500), as amended.

Clean Water Action Plan (CWAP): Administration initiative announced in February 1998 intended to coordinate federal efforts to address the nation's remaining water quality challenges.

Comprehensive Nutrient Management Plan (CNMP): A plan that identifies actions or priorities that will be followed to meet defined nutrient management goals at an agricultural operation. CNMPs may address, as necessary, feed management, manure handling and storage, land application of manure, land management, record keeping and other utilization options.

Concentrated animal feeding operation (CAFO): An animal feeding operation that meets EPA regulatory definitions, where more than 1,000 animal units are confined at the facility; or more than 300 animal units are confined at the facilities and (1) pollutants are discharged into navigable waters through a manmade ditch, flushing system, or other similar manmade device, or (2) pollutants are discharged directly into waters that originate outside of and pass over, across, or through the facility or come into direct contact with the confined animals.

National Pollutant Discharge Elimination System (NPDES): The principal discharge permit program of the CWA, authorized in section 402 of the law. NPDES permits, issued by EPA or authorized states, are required in order to discharge from a point source into waters of the United States. NPDES permits contain limits on what can be discharged, monitoring and reporting requirements.

Nonpoint source: Under the CWA, sources that do not meet the definition of point source, generally including diffuse runoff that does not enter the nation's waters from a discernible, confined and discrete conveyance. Nonpoint source pollution is the by-product of a variety of land use practices, including farming, timber harvesting, mining, and construction. It also results when rainfall and snowmelt wash pollutants in urban areas into sewer systems and storm drains. Nonpoint sources are not subject to NPDES permit requirements. Under this law, they are managed primarily through the Act's section 319 program, which requires states to assess the extent to which nonpoint sources cause water quality problems and develop management programs to address them.

Point source: Under the CWA, means any discernible, confined and discrete conveyance, such as pipes, ditches, channels and tunnels, from which pollutants are or may be discharged. Point sources are subject to NPDES requirements. The term does include CAFOs but does not include agricultural stormwater discharges and return flows from irrigated agriculture.

Total Maximum Daily Load (TMDL): A quantitative assessment of water quality problems, pollution sources, and pollutant reductions needed to restore and protect a river, stream, lake, or coastal waterbody, as required by section 303(d) of the CWA.

Watershed approach: An approach to resource management that focuses on hydrologically defined drainage basins (watersheds) as the areas of study, rather than areas defined by political or other boundaries. The watershed protection approach identifies the primary threats to human and ecosystem health within a watershed and takes a comprehensive, integrated approach to solutions and actions.

TIMELINE OF IDENTIFIED ACTIVITIES AND EVENTS
IN THE AFO STRATEGY AND TMDL PROGRAM

February 1998: President and Vice President released the Clean Water Action Plan

March 1999: EPA and USDA issued the Unified National Strategy for Animal Feeding Operations *(AFO Strategy)*[36]

May 1999: USDA/NRCS issued the Policy for Nutrient Management and revised conservation practice standards for nutrient management *(AFO Strategy)*

August 1999: EPA issued draft guidance manual for NPDES permits for CAFOs *(AFO Strategy)*

EPA proposed revised regulations for the TMDL program **December 1999**: USDA issued draft technical guidance for developing comprehensive nutrient management plans *(AFO Strategy)*

2000-2005: Round I CAFO permitting *(AFO Strategy)*

January 2000: EPA and states should issue general permits for large CAFOs with significant manure production. Permits expire in 5 years. *(AFO Strategy)*

Jan. 22, 2000: Public comment period on proposed TMDL regulations closed

July 11, 2000: EPA promulgated comprehensive revisions to existing TMDL regulations

December 2000: EPA and USDA will develop a coordinated technical transfer and education plan to disseminate results of AFO-related research *(AFO Strategy)*

EPA and USDA will develop a Virtual Center to serve as a single point of reference regarding research topics *(AFO Strategy)*

Dec. 15, 2000: EPA proposed revised effluent guidelines and permitting regulations for poultry, swine, beef and dairy cattle. (EPA is under court order) *(AFO Strategy)*

May 15, 2001: EPA shall submit to Congress a cost and capability assessment report on the AFO strategy *(EPA FY2000 appropriations, P.L. 106-74, H.Rept. 106-379)*

2001: CAFO inspections–EPA and states should inspect all CAFOs in priority areas by end of FY2001 *(AFO Strategy)*

Apr. 1, 2002: States must provide EPA and the public with the methodology used to compile 303(d) lists of impaired waters. Similar submission is due on April

---

[36] Based on schedules and information contained in the Unified National Strategy for Animal Feeding Operations, issued March 1999.

1 of each listing year – 4 years. *(TMDL[37])*

Dec. 15, 2002: EPA will issue revised effluent limitation guidelines and permitting regulations for poultry, swine, beef and dairy cattle (EPA is under court order) *(AFO Strategy)*

2002: EPA and states should issue permits for smaller CAFOs with unacceptable conditions or significant contributions to water quality impairments by the end of this year. Permits expire in 5 years. *(AFO Strategy)*

2003: CAFO inspections–EPA and states should inspect all other CAFOs by end of FY2003 *(AFO Strategy)*

Large CAFOs that were issued general permits in 2000 should develop and fully implement Comprehensive Nutrient Management Plans (CNMPs) no later than the end of this year *(AFO Strategy)*

Apr. 1, 2004: States must submit lists of impaired waters for EPA approval. This list must include schedule for developing TMDLs that provides for establishment of TMDLs within 10 years (a 5-year extension is possible). Subsequent listing submissions are due every 4 years. *(TMDL)*

2005: Smaller CAFOs that were issued permits in 2002 should develop and begin implementation of CNMPs by the end of this year *(AFO Strategy)*

2005-2010: Round II CAFO permitting by EPA and states to reissue general permits and individual permits as they expire, incorporating new requirements resulting from revision of CAFO permit regulations and effluent limitation guidelines plus refinements to site-specific CNMPs and any additional requirements needed to achieve water quality goals (i.e., state water quality standards for nutrients, TMDLs) *(AFO Strategy)*

---

[37] Based on revised regulations for the TMDL program issued in July 2000.

GUIDE TO BOOKS

1992 statewide water quality assessment section 305(b) report.
Published/Created: [Olympia? Wash.]: State of Washington, Dept. of Ecology,
Water Quality Program, [1992]
Related Names: Washington (State). Dept. of Ecology. Water Quality Program.
Description: ix, 245, [289] p.: maps; 28 cm.
Notes: "This assessment report has been prepared to fulfill the State of
Washington's obligation under Section 305(b) of the federal Clean Water Act."
"April 1992."
Subjects: Water quality--Washington (State)
Series: Publication (Washington (State). Dept. of Ecology); #92-04.
Variant Series: Publication; #92-04
LC Classification: TD224.W2 A15 1992
Dewey Class No.: 363.739/42/09797 21

1998 update: the Clean Water Act: May 12, 1998, an ABA satellite seminar / co-
sponsored by the American Bar Association, Section of Natural Resources,
Energy, and Environmental Law, Center for Continuing Legal Education, Water
Environment Federation; in cooperation with U.S. Environmental Protection
Agency.
Published/Created: [Chicago]: The Association, c1998.
Related Names: American Bar Association.
Description: 1 v. (various pagings): ill., forms; 28 cm.
Subjects: Water--Pollution--Law and legislation--United States.
LC Classification: KF3790.Z9 A135 1998
Dewey Class No.: 344.73/046343 21

305(b) technical report for Oklahoma / prepared by the Oklahoma State Department
of Health; coordinated by the Pollution Control Coordinating Board.
Published/Created: Oklahoma City: The Department,
Related Names: Oklahoma. State Dept. of Health. Oklahoma. Pollution Control

Coordinating Board.
Description: v.: ill., maps; 28 cm.
Current Frequency: Biennial
ISSN: 0740-9923
Notes: " ... produced as a result of the Clean water act, Public Law 92-500, Section 305(b) ..." Description based on: Water years 1980-1981.
SERBIB/SERLOC merged record
Subjects: Water-supply--Oklahoma--Periodicals. Water--Pollution--Oklahoma--Periodicals.
LC Classification: TD224.O5 A57
Dewey Class No.: 363.7/3942/09766 19

Adler, Robert W., 1955-
The Clean Water Act 20 years later / Robert W. Adler, Jessica C. Landman, and Diane M. Cameron.
Published/Created: Washington, D.C.: Island Press, c1993.
Related Names: Landman, Jessica C. Cameron, Diane M.
Related Titles: Clean Water Act twenty years later.
Description: xii, 320 p.: ill.; 24 cm.
ISBN: 1559632658 (cloth: alk. paper): 1559632666 (pbk.: alk. paper) :
Notes: Includes bibliographical references and index.
Subjects: United States. Federal Water Pollution Control Act. Water quality--United States. Water quality management--United States--History.
LC Classification: TD223 .A4663 1993
Dewey Class No.: 363.73/946/0973

Alberta's Clean Water Act.
Published/Created: Edmonton, Alta.: Environment Council of Alberta, [1985]
Related Names: Lilley, John. Environment Council of Alberta. Alberta. Alberta Environment.
Description: iii, 101 p.; 28 cm.
Contents: Conclusions and recommendations of the review of the Clean Water Act: report of the Environment Council of Alberta to the Minister of the Environment -- Review of the Clean Water Act: staff report / prepared by John Lilley.
Notes: "March 1985." Includes bibliographies.
Subjects: Water--Pollution--Law and legislation--Alberta.
LC Classification: KEA422.W3 A73 1985
Dewey Class No.: 344.7123/046343 347.1230446343 19

Anderson, Jack.
Historical changes in land use/land cover: a case study of two subwatersheds within the reservoir watershed: a report prepared for the Reservoir Watershed Protection Program / Jack Anderson.
Published/Created: Baltimore, Md. (601 N. Howard St., Baltimore 21201):

Baltimore Metropolitan Council, [1992]
Related Names: Reservoir Watershed Protection Program (Md.) Baltimore
Metropolitan Council.
Description: 1 v. (various pagings): ill.; 28 cm.
Notes: "September 1992." "This report was funded, in part, by a Clean Water Act
Section 604 (b) grant provided by the Maryland Department of the Environment."
Includes bibliographical references.
Subjects: Watershed management--Maryland. Reservoirs--Maryland. Land use--
Maryland.
LC Classification: TC424.M3 A83 1992
Dewey Class No.: 333.91/16/09752 20

Arizona's ... water quality limited waters list: Arizona's 303(d) list.
Published/Created: Phoenix, Ariz.: Arizona Dept. of Environmental Quality,
Related Names: Arizona. Dept. of Environmental Quality.
Description: v.: map; 28 cm.
Current Frequency: Biennial
Notes: Prepared in fulfillment of section 303(d) of the Federal Clean Water Act.
Description based on: 1998; title from cover.
Subjects: Water quality management--Arizona--Periodicals.
LC Classification: TD224.A7 A94

Bauer, Steve.
Aquatic habitat indicators and their application to water quality objectives within
the Clean Water Act / Stephen B. Bauer and Stephen C. Ralph.
Published/Created: Seattle, WA: United States Environmental Protection Agency,
Region 10; Moscow, ID: Idaho Water Resources Research Institute, University of
Idaho, 1999.
Related Names: Ralph, Stephen C. United States. Environmental Protection
Agency. Region X. Idaho Water Resources Research Institute.
Description: viii, 99 p.: ill., maps; 28 cm.
Notes: "This document was developed for US Environmental Protection Agency,
Region 10, Seattle Washington, with the Idaho Water Resources Institute,
University of Idaho." Includes bibliographical references (p. 70-77).
Subjects: United States. Federal Water Pollution Control Act. Indicators
(Biology) Water quality management--United States. Water quality--United
States. Water--Pollution--Law and legislation--United States.
LC Classification: QH541.15.I5 B28 1999

Chase, Jim.
The state of New Hampshire's estuaries / Jim Chase and Lorraine Merrill, authors.
Published/Created: Portsmouth, N.H.: New Hampshire Estuaries Project, [2000]
Related Names: Merrill, Lorraine. New Hampshire Estuaries Project.
Description: 46 p.: ill. (some col.), maps (some col.); 28 cm.
Notes: Cover title. "November, 2000"--P. [2] of cover. Funded in part by a grant

from the NH Office of State Planning, New Hampshire Estuaries Project, as
authorized by the U.S. Environmental Protection Agency pursuant to Section 320
of the Clean Water Act.
Subjects: New Hampshire Estuaries Project. Estuarine ecology--New Hampshire.
Estuarine health--New Hampshire. Estuarine area conservation--New Hampshire.
LC Classification: QH105.N4 C48 2000
Dewey Class No.: 333.91/64 21

Clean Water Act / by Mark Ryan, editor.
    Edition Information: 2nd ed.
    Published/Created: Chicago: Section of Environment, Energy, and Resources,
    American Bar Association, c2003.
    Projected Pub. Date: 0305
    Related Names: Ryan, Mark, 1957- American Bar Association. Section of
    Environment, Energy, and Resources.
    Related Titles: [Clean Water Act handbook.
    Description: p. cm.
    ISBN: 1590312171
    Contents: Overview of the Clean Water Act / Theodore L. Garrett -- Water
    pollution control under the National Pollutant Discharge Elimination System /
    Karen M. McGaffey -- NPDES permit application and issuance procedures /
    Randy Hill -- Publicly Owned Treatment Works (POTWs) / Alexandra Dapolito
    Dunn -- Pretreatment and indirect dischargers / Corinne A. Goldstein -- Wetlands:
    Section 404 / Sylvia Quast, Steven T. Miano -- Oil and hazardous substance
    spills: Section 311 / David G. Dickman -- "Wet Weather" regulations: Control of
    stormwater and discharges from concentrated animal feeding operations and other
    facilities / Randy Hill, David Allnutt -- Nonpoint source pollution control /
    Edward B. Witte, David P. Ross -- TMDLs: Section 303(d) / Laurie K. Beale,
    Karin Sheldon -- Enforcement: Section 309 / Beth S. Ginsberg ... [et al.] --
    Judicial review: Section 509 / Karen M. McGaffey.
    Notes: Rev. ed. of: The Clean Water Act handbook / Parthenia B. Evans, editor.
    Includes index.
    Subjects: United States. Federal Water Pollution Control Act. Water--Pollution--
    Law and legislation--United States.
    LC Classification: KF3790 .C545 2003
    Dewey Class No.: 344.73/046343 21

Clean water act corporate counsel retreat and information exchange: course materials /
    American Bar Association, Section of Natural Resources, Energy and
    Environmental Law.
    Published/Created: Chicago, Ill.: American Bar Association, 1993-
    Related Names: American Bar Association. Section of Natural Resources,
    Energy, and Environmental Law.
    Description: v.; 28 cm. June 24, 1993-
    Current Frequency: Annual

Continued by: Annual clean water act corporate counsel retreat and information exchange (DLC) 96640319
Notes: SERBIB/SERLOC merged record
Subjects: Water--Pollution--Law and legislation--United States.
LC Classification: KF3790.Z9 C585
Dewey Class No.: 344.73/046343 21

Clean Water Act permit guidance manual / Russell S. Frye ... [et al.].
Published/Created: New York, N.Y.: Executive Enterprises Publications Co, c1984.
Related Names: Frye, Russell S.
Description: xvii, 644 p.; 28 cm.
ISBN: 0880571365 (pbk.)
Notes: Includes index.
Subjects: Water--Pollution--Law and legislation--United States. Environmental law--United States.
LC Classification: KF3790 .C55 1984
Dewey Class No.: 344.73/046343 347.30446343 19

Clean Water Act Section 303(d) list: Illinois' submittal for 1998.
Published/Created: Springfield, Ill.: Illinois Environmental Protection Agency, Bureau of Water, Division of Water Pollution Control, Planning Section, [1998]
Related Names: Illinois. Bureau of Water. Illinois. Division of Water Pollution Control. Planning Section.
Description: 1 v. (various pagings): maps (some col.); 28 cm.
Summary: The purpose of this report is to fulfill the requirements set forth in Section 303(d) of the Federal Clean Water Act (CWA) and the Water Quality Planning and Management regulation at 40 CFR Part 130. This report is submitted to the U.S. Environmental Protection Agency (USEPA) for review and approval of Illinois' list of water quality limited waters. It provides the state's supporting documentation required by 40 CFR Part 130.7 (b)(6) and rationale in fulfilling Section 303(d) requirements. Illinois has elected to provide its submittal of Section 303(d) requirements as a separate document as opposed to inclusion in the state's biennial 305(b) report.
Notes: "April 1, 1998"--Cover. "IEPA/BOW/97-023."--Cover.
Subjects: United States. Federal Water Pollution Control Act. Water quality management--Illinois. Water--Pollution--Law and legislation--Illinois.
LC Classification: TD224.I3 .C58 1998
Dewey Class No.: 363.739/456/09773 21

Clean Water Act update / Russell S. Frye ... [et al.].
Published/Created: New York, N.Y.: Executive Enterprises Publications, c1987.
Related Names: Frye, Russell S. United States. Water Quality Act of 1987. 1987.
Related Titles: [Clean Water Act permit guidance manual.
Description: iii, 198 p.; 28 cm.

ISBN: 0880578319 (pbk.)
Notes: Supplement and update of: Clean Water Act permit guidance manual.
Subjects: Water--Pollution--Law and legislation--United States.
LC Classification: KF3790 .C55 1984 Suppl.
Dewey Class No.: 344.73/046343 347.30446343 19

Clean Water Act: corporate counsel retreat and information exchange: course
    materials, June 24, 1993, Chicago, Illinois.
    Published/Created: [Chicago]: American Bar Association, Section of Natural
    Resources, Energy, and Environmental Law, c1993.
    Related Names: American Bar Association. Section of Natural Resources,
    Energy, and Environmental Law.
    Description: 1 v. (various pagings); 28 cm.
    Subjects: Water--Pollution--Law and legislation--United States.
    LC Classification: KF3790.A2 C57 1993
    Dewey Class No.: 344.73/046343 347.30446343 20

Clean Water Act: law and regulation: October 23-25, 2002, Washington, D.C.: ALI-
    ABA course of study materials / cosponsored by the ABA Section of
    Environment, Energy, and Resources and the Environmental Law Institute.
    Published/Created: Philadelphia, PA (4025 Chestnut St., Philadelphia 19104-
    3099): American Law Institute-American Bar Association Committee on
    Continuing Professional Education, c2002.
    Description: xxi, 280 p.: ill.; 28 cm.
    Notes: "SH041."
    Subjects: United States. Federal Water Pollution Control Act. Water--Pollution--
    Law and legislation--United States.
    LC Classification: KF3790.Z9 C+

Colorado. Dept. of Health. Water Quality Control Division.
    Water quality in Colorado / Water Quality Control Division, Colorado
    Department of Health.
    Published/Created: Denver, Colo.: The Division, 1988.
    Related Titles: Colorado water quality.
    Description: 1 v. (various pagings): maps; 28 cm.
    Notes: Cover title: Colorado water quality. "December 1988." "Prepared in
    fulfillment of Section 305(b) of the Clean Water Act of 1977 (P.L. 95-217."
    Colorado state doc. no.: HE7/150.2/QU2/1988. Includes bibliographical
    references.
    Subjects: Water--Pollution--Colorado. Water quality--Colorado. Water quality
    management--Colorado.
    LC Classification: TD224.C7 C63 1988c

Combined sewer overflow policy: federal Clean Water Act & Pa. clean streams law
    regulation comes to local government.

Published/Created: [Harrisburg, Pa.] (104 S. St., Harrisburg 17108-1027):
Pennsylvania Bar Institute, c1995.
Related Names: Pennsylvania Bar Institute.
Description: ix, 114 p.: ill.; 28 cm.
Notes: Includes bibliographical references (p. 59-60).
Subjects: Sewage disposal--Law and legislation--Pennsylvania. Water--Pollution-
-Law and legislation--Pennsylvania. Combined sewer overflows--United States.
Series: PBI (Series); no. 1995-999.
Variant Series: PBI; no. 1995-999
LC Classification: KFP359.S4 C66 1995
Dewey Class No.: 344.748/04622 21

Compensating for wetland losses under the Clean Water Act / Committee on
Mitigating Wetland Losses, Board on Environmental Studies and Toxicology,
Water Science and Technology Board, Division on Earth and Life Studies,
National Research Council.
Published/Created: Washington, D.C.: National Academy Press, c2001.
Related Names: National Research Council (U.S.). Committee on Mitigating
Wetland Losses.
Description: xxiii, 322 p.: ill.; 24 cm.
ISBN: 0309074320 (hardcover)
Notes: Includes bibliographical references (p. 169-186) and index.
Subjects: Wetlands--Law and legislation--United States. Wetland conservation--
Government policy--United States. Wetland mitigation banking--United States.
LC Classification: KF5624 .C66 2001
Dewey Class No.: 346.7304/6918 21

Connecticut. Water Compliance Unit.
State of Connecticut water quality management plan, October 1, 1984: pursuant
to sections 106 and 303 of the Federal Clean Water Act / Connecticut Department
of Environmental Protection, Water Compliance Unit.
Published/Created: [Hartford]: The Unit, [1984]
Description: 81 p.: ill.; 28 cm.
Subjects: Water quality management--Government policy--Connecticut.
LC Classification: HD1694.C8 C8 1984
Dewey Class No.: 363.7/39456/09746 19

Environmental regulation essentials.
Published/Created: New York, N.Y.: Executive Enterprises, c1994-
Description: v.; 28 cm. 1993/94-
Current Frequency: Annual
ISSN: 1069-5222
Cancel/Invalid LCCN: sn 93002543
Notes: Title from publisher's note. Vol. for 1993/94 comprised of 11 parts issued
in 2 looseleaf vols.: Vol. 1: Book 1, National Environmental Policy Act (NEPA);

Book 2, Clean Air Act (CAA); Book 3, Clean Water Act (CWA); Book 4, Resource Conservation and Recovery Act (RCRA); Book 5, Comprehensive Environmental Response, Compensation and Liability Act (CERCLA); Book 6, Emergency Planning and Community Right-to-Know Act (EPCRA); Vol. 2: Book 7, Toxic Substances Control Act (TSCA); Book 8, Occupational Safety and Health Act (OSHA); Book 9, Compliance auditing; Book 10, Environmental acronyms and glossary; Book 11, Environmental directory. SERBIB/SERLOC merged record
Subjects: Environmental law--Hazardous substances--Law and legislation--Environmental protection--United States--Periodicals.
LC Classification: KF3775.A15 E592
Dewey Class No.: 344.73/046/05 347.3044605 20

Gallagher, Lynn M. (Lynn Monk)
Clean water handbook / Lynn M. Gallagher, Leonard A. Miller.
Edition Information: 2nd ed.
Published/Created: Rockville, Md.: Government Institutes, 1996.
Related Names: Miller, Leonard A. United States. Federal Water Pollution Control Act.
Description: x, 439 p.: ill.; 28 cm.
ISBN: 086587512X
Notes: Includes Clean Water Act. Includes index.
Subjects: Water--Pollution--Law and legislation--Environmental permits—U.S.
LC Classification: KF3790 .G35 1996
Dewey Class No.: 344.73/046343 21

Houck, Oliver A.
The Clean Water Act TMDL program: law, policy, and implementation / Oliver A. Houck.
Published/Created: Washington, D.C.: Environmental Law Institute, 1999.
Description: x, 388 p.; 23 cm.
ISBN: 0911937994
Notes: Includes bibliographical references.
Subjects: Water--Pollution--Law and legislation--United States.
LC Classification: KF3790 .H68 1999
Dewey Class No.: 344.73/046343 21

Illinois water quality report (Clean Water Act, section 305(b) report): water resource assessment information based on data collected through ... / State of Illinois, Environmental Protection Agency, Bureau of Water.
Published/Created: Springfield, IL: The Bureau, 2002-
Description: v.
Current Frequency: Biennial
Notes: Description based on: 2002.

Impact of animal waste lagoons on ground water quality: section 319, Clean Water
    Act, Grant Year FY 94: final report / Division of Water Quality, Groundwater
    Section.
    Published/Created: [Raleigh, N.C.]: The Section, [1998]
    Description: 131 p.: ill., map, plans; 28 cm.
    Notes: Cover title. "June, 1998." Includes bibliographical references (p. 97-100).
    Subjects: Sewage lagoons--North Carolina. Farm manure--Environmental
    aspects--North Carolina. Groundwater--North Carolina--Quality. Groundwater--
    Sampling--North Carolina.
    LC Classification: TD746.5 .I48 1998
    Dewey Class No.: 628.1/6846 21
    Govt. Doc. No.: C26 9:L177 ncdocs

Library of Congress. Environmental Policy Division.
    A legislative history of the Water pollution control act amendments of 1972,
    together with a section-by-section index.
    Published/Created: Washington, U.S. Govt. Print. Off., 1973-78.
    Description: 4 v. 23 cm.
    Notes: At head of title: 93d Congress, 1st session [-95th Congress, 2d session]
    Committee print. "Serial no. 93-1" and "Serial no. 95-14." "Printed for the use of
    the Committee on Public Works." Vols. 3-4 have title: A legislative history of the
    Clean water act of 1977. "An Act to amend the Federal water pollution control
    act": v. 1, p. 3-91. Includes index.
    Subjects: United States. Laws, statutes, etc. Federal water pollution control act
    amendments of 1972.
    LC Classification: KF3787.122 .A15 1973
    Dewey Class No.: 344.73/046343/09 19

Maine. Land Use Regulation Commission.
    A survey of erosion and sedimentation problems associated with logging in
    Maine / submitted to Maine Department of Environmental Protection by Maine
    Land Use Regulation Commission, May, 1979.
    Published/Created: [Augusta, Me.]: The Commission, [1979]
    Related Names: Born, John W. Maine. Dept. of Environmental Protection.
    Description: 56 p.: ill.; 28 cm.
    Notes: Cover title. J. W. Born, principal author. "A water quality planning report
    funded by section 208 of the Federal clean water act (PL 92-500)" Bibliography:
    p. 43.
    Subjects: Lumbering--Environmental aspects--Maine. Water--Pollution--Maine.
    Sediment transport--Maine. Soil erosion--Maine.
    LC Classification: TD428.F67 M34 1979
    Dewey Class No.: 333.75/16/09741 19

Management of hard to handle wastes in Vermont: a discussion paper / prepared by
    the Vermont Agency of Natural Resources, Department of Environmental

Conservation, Environmental Assistance Division with funding assistance from
the United States Environmental Protection Agency for nonpoint source projects
initiated under Section 319 of the Federal Clean Water Act.
Published/Created: [Vermont]: The Agency, [1998]
Related Names: Vermont. Dept. of Environmental Conservation. Environmental
Assistance Division.
Description: 23 p.; 28 cm.
Notes: Cover title. "May 1998." Includes bibliographical references (p. 21-23).
Subjects: Hazardous wastes--Vermont--Management.
LC Classification: TD1042.V5 M35 1998
Dewey Class No.: 363.72/87/09743 21

Maryland. Office of Environmental Programs.
Maryland water quality inventory: a report on the progress toward meeting the
goals of the Clean Water Act / Office of Environmental Programs, Department of
Health and Mental Hygiene.
Published/Created: [Baltimore, Md.]: The Office, 1982-
Description: v.: maps; 28 cm. 1982-
Current Frequency: Biennial
Notes: SERBIB/SERLOC merged record
Subjects: Water quality management--Maryland--Periodicals. Water quality--
Maryland. Water quality management--Maryland.
LC Classification: TD224.M3 M286a
Dewey Class No.: 363.7/394/5609752 19

Minnesota Pollution Control Agency.
Minnesota nonpoint source management progress in federal fiscal year 1992: the
1992 report to U.S. Environmental Protection Agency / submitted by the
Minnesota Pollution Control Agency, pursuant to Section 319(h) of the Clean
Water Act.
Published/Created: [St. Paul]: The Agency, [1992]
Related Names: United States. Environmental Protection Agency.
Description: 238 p.; 28 cm.
Subjects: Water quality management--Minnesota. Nonpoint source pollution--
Minnesota.
LC Classification: TD224.M6 M577 1992
Dewey Class No.: 363.73/946/09776 20

Montana. Water Quality Bureau.
Water quality in Montana-1980 / prepared for Environmental Protection Agency,
Region VIII, Denver, Colorado, pursuant to the Clean water act, section 305(b)
by Water Quality Bureau, Environmental Science Division, Department of Health
and Environmental Sciences, with assistance from Montana EPA Office.
Published/Created: [Helena]: The Bureau, 1980.
Related Names: United States. Environmental Protection Agency. Region VIII.

Description: 247, [7] p.: maps (1 fold. col. in pocket); 28 cm.
Notes: Includes bibliographical references.
Subjects: Water quality--Montana.
LC Classification: TD224.M9 M68 1980
Dewey Class No.: 363.7/3942/09786 19

National Water Conference (1982: Philadelphia, Pa.)
Proceedings of the National Water Conference: water quality and the Clean
Water Act, January 26 and 27, 1982 / [James Wilson, editor]; sponsored by the
Academy of Natural Sciences, the American Water Works Association, the Water
Pollution Control Federation.
Published/Created: Philadelphia, Pa.: The Academy, 1982.
Related Names: Wilson, James, 1947-
Description: 216 p.: ill.; 21 cm.
Notes: Cover title. Includes bibliographical references.
Subjects: Water--Pollution--Law and legislation--United States Congresses.
Water quality--United States--Congresses.
LC Classification: KF3790.A2 N37 1982
Dewey Class No.: 344.73/046343 347.30446343 19

Nebraska Nonpoint Source Management Program.
Annual NPS report: prepared pursuant to section 319 of the Clean Water Act /
Nebraska Nonpoint Source Management Program.
Published/Created: Lincoln, Neb.: Nebraska Dept. of Environmental Control,
Water Quality Division,
Related Names: Nebraska. Water Quality Division.
Description: v.; 28 cm.
Current Frequency: Annual
Notes: Description based on: Sept. 1991. SERBIB/SERLOC merged record
Subjects: Nebraska Nonpoint Source Management Program--Periodicals. Water
quality management--Nebraska--Planning--Periodicals. Water--Pollution--
Nebraska--Government policy Periodicals.
LC Classification: WMLC 93/5527
Govt. Doc. No.: E6900 B006- nbdocs

New Jersey 1988 state water quality inventory reort: a report on the status of water
quality in New Jersey pursuant to the New Jersey Water Pollution Control Act
and Section 305(b) of the Federal Clean Water Act / State of New Jersey,
Department of Environmental Protection, Division of Water Resources, Bureau
of Water Quality Planning.
Published/Created: Trenton, N.J.: The Bureau, [1988]
Description: 1 v. (various pagings): ill.; 28 cm.
LC Classification: IN PROCESS (ONLINE)

New Mexico nonpoint source pollution water quality assessment: a report prepared
pursuant to Section 319 of the Federal Clean Water Act.
Published/Created: Santa Fe, N.M.: New Mexico Water Quality Control
Commission, [1988]
Related Names: New Mexico Water Quality Control Commission.
Description: iii, 75 p.: ill., maps; 28 cm.
Notes: Cover title. "September 1988." "EID-WPC-88/2." Bibliography: p. 71-73.
Subjects: Water quality--New Mexico.
LC Classification: MLCM 91/10881 (T)

New Mexico. Water Quality Control Commission.
State of New Mexico water quality status summary: a report prepared for
submission to the Congress of the United States / by the State of New Mexico,
pursuant to section 305(b) of the Federal Clean Water Act.
Published/Created: Santa Fe, N.M. (Post Office Box 968, Santa Fe, N.M. 87503):
New Mexico Water Quality Control Commission, [1980]
Related Names: United States. Congress.
Description: ii, 69, [25] p.: maps; 28 cm.
Notes: "May 1980."
Subjects: Water quality--New Mexico.
LC Classification: TD224.N6 N48 1980
Dewey Class No.: 363.7/3942/09789 19

New York State water quality ... / Prepared by Bureau of Monitoring & Assessment,
Division of Water, New York State Department of Environmental Conservation.
Published/Created: Albany, N.Y.: The Bureau,
Related Names: New York (State). Division of Water. Bureau of Monitoring and
Assessment. New York (State). Division of Water. Bureau of Watershed
Assessment and Research.
Description: v.; 28 cm.
Current Frequency: Biennial
Cancel/Invalid LCCN: sn 89039984
Notes: "Submitted pursuant to Section 305(b) of the Federal Clean Water Act
Amendments of 1977 (PL95-217)." Description based on: Apr. 1988. Issued by:
Bureau of Watershed Assessment and Research, May 1996- SERBIB/SERLOC
merged record
Additional Form Avail.: Electronic version (Scanned image TIFF format)
available via New York State Library WWW site.
Subjects: Water quality--New York (State)--Periodicals.
Series: DEC publication.
Variant Series: <1988->: DEC publication
LC Classification: TD224.N7 N48
Dewey Class No.: 363.739/456/09747 21
Govt. Doc. No.: WAT 120-3 NEWYS 89-14721 nydocs

North Dakota nonpoint source management report: prepared to fulfill the requirements
   of Section 319 of the Clean Water Act / by the North Dakota State Department of
   Health and Consolidated Laboratories, Division of Water Supply and Pollution
   Control.
   Cover Title: North Dakota Nonpoint Source Pollution Management Program.
   Published/Created: [Bismarck, N.D.: The Division, 1993]
   Related Names: North Dakota. Division of Water Supply and Pollution Control.
   Description: iv leaves, 132 p.: maps; 28 cm.
   Notes: "September 1993"--Cover.
   Subjects: Water quality management--North Dakota. Nonpoint source pollution--
   North Dakota.
   LC Classification: TD224.N9 N665 1993
   Dewey Class No.: 363.73/945/09784 20

Oklahoma's 1990 water quality assessment report: prepared pursuant to Section
   305(b) of the Federal Clean Water Act / prepared for the Oklahoma Pollution
   Control Coordinating Board, by the Oklahoma Department of Pollution Control.
   Published/Created: [Oklahoma City, OK] (1000 NE 10th St., Rm 1114,
   Oklahoma City 73152): The Dept., [1990]
   Related Names: Oklahoma. Pollution Control Coordinating Board. Oklahoma.
   Dept. of Pollution Control.
   Description: 57 p.; 28 cm.
   Notes: Cover title. Includes bibliographical references (p. 56)
   Subjects: Water quality--Oklahoma. Water quality management--Oklahoma.
   LC Classification: TD224.O5 O38 1990
   Dewey Class No.: 363.73/9456/09766 20

Oregon. Dept. of Environmental Quality.
   Oregon's ... water quality status assessment report.
   Published/Created: Portland, Or.: Dept. of Environmental Quality,
   Description: v.: maps; 29 cm. None published for 1996.
   Current Frequency: Biennial
   Continues: Oregon. Dept. of Environmental Quality. Oregon ... water quality
   program assessment and program plan for fiscal year ... (OCoLC)25376354
   Notes: Report prepared to fulfill the requirements of Section 305(b) of the Clean
   Water Act. Description based on: 1992. SERBIB/SERLOC merged record
   Subjects: Oregon. Dept. of Environmental Quality. Water Quality Division--
   Periodicals. Water quality--Oregon--Periodicals.
   LC Classification: TD224.O7 O68a
   Dewey Class No.: 363.73/942/09797 20
   Govt. Doc. No.: EQ.3W29 ordocs

Reauthorization of the Clean Water Act: 1983, 98th Congress, 1st session.
   Published/Created: Washington: American Enterprise Institute for Public Policy
   Research, [1983]

Related Names: American Enterprise Institute for Public Policy Research.
Description: 48 p.; 26 cm.
ISBN: 084470248X (pbk.)
Notes: "July 1983"--T.p. verso. Includes bibliographical references.
Subjects: Water--Pollution--Law and legislation--United States. Sewage disposal plants--Law and legislation--United States.
Series: AEI legislative analyses; 98th Congress, no. 33.
Variant Series: AEI legislative analyses; no. 33, 98th Congress
LC Classification: KF3790 .R4 1983
Dewey Class No.: 353.0082/325 19

Regional Planning Council (Md.)
Water quality management plan for the Baltimore metropolitan region, 1981: amended plan adopted by Regional Planning Council, 208 Coordinating Committee, and member local governments, 1980-81.
Published/Created: Baltimore, Md.: The Council, [1982]
Description: 1 v. (various pagings): ill.; 28 cm.
Notes: "The work on this plan was supported in part by a grant from the U.S. Environmental Protection Agency under Section 208 Public Law 92-500, the Clean Water Act."
Subjects: Water quality management--Government policy--Maryland Baltimore Metropolitan Area.
LC Classification: HC108.B2 R44 1982
Dewey Class No.: 333.91/22/097526 19

State of Texas 1998 Clean Water Act, section 303(d) list and schedule for development of total maximum daily loads / prepared by the Water Quality Division.
Published/Created: Austin, Tex.: Texas Natural Resource Conservation Commission, [1998]
Related Names: Texas Natural Resource Conservation Commission. Water Quality Division.
Description: 1 v. (various pagings): maps; 28 cm.
Notes: "June 26, 1998." "SFR-58."
Subjects: Water--Pollution--Total maximum daily load--Texas. Water quality--Standards--Texas. Water--Pollution--Law and legislation--United States.
LC Classification: TD224.T4 S72 1998
Dewey Class No.: 363.739/46/09764 21
Govt. Doc. No.: N330.8 C58WALI 1998 txdocs

Structure and effectiveness of the state's water quality programs: section 303(d) of the Federal Clean Water Act and total maximum daily loads (TMDLs): report to the legislature, pursuant to AB 982 of 1999.
Published/Created: Sacramento, Calif.: State Water Resources Control Board, California Environmental Protection Agency, [2002]

Related Names: California Environmental Protection Agency. State Water
Resources Control Board.
Description: 1 v. (various pagings): ill.; 28 cm.
Notes: Cover title. "February 2002."
Additional Form Avail.: Also available via the World Wide Web.
Subjects: Water quality management--California--Evaluation. Environmental
agencies--California--Evaluation.
LC Classification: TD224.C3 S75 2002

The Clean Water Act as amended by the Water Quality Act of 1987.
Published/Created: Washington, D.C.: U.S. G.P.O.: For sale by the Supt. of
Docs., Congressional Sales Office, U.S. G.P.O., 1988.
Related Names: United States. Congress. Senate. Committee on Environment and
Public Works.
Related Titles: Clean Water Act.
Description: iv, 214 p.; 24 cm.
Notes: At head of title: 100th Congress, 2d session. Committee print. "Printed for
the use of the Senate Committee on Environment and Public Works." Distributed
to some depository libraries in microfiche. Shipping list no.: 88-195-P. "March
1988." Item 1045-A, 1045-B (microfiche) Includes bibliographical references.
Subjects: Water--Pollution--Law and legislation--United States. Federal aid to
water quality management--United States.
Series: S. prt.; 100-91
LC Classification: KF3786.A55 C55 1988
NAL Class No.: KF3790.Z9C5
Dewey Class No.: 344.73/046343/02632 347.3044634302632 20
Govt. Doc. No.: Y 4.P 96/10:S.prt.100-91

The Clean Water Act handbook / Parthenia B. Evans, editor.
Published/Created: Chicago, Ill.: SONREEL, Section of Natural Resources,
Energy and Environmental Law, American Bar Association, c1994.
Related Names: Evans, Parthenia B. American Bar Association. Section of
Natural Resources, Energy, and Environmental Law.
Description: xxx, 282 p.; 23 cm.
ISBN: 157073030X
Notes: Includes bibliographical references and index.
Subjects: United States. Federal Water Pollution Control Act. Water--Pollution--
Law and legislation--United States.
LC Classification: KF3790 .C545 1994
Dewey Class No.: 344.73/046343 347.30446343 20

The Clean water act showing changes made by the 1977 amendments.
Published/Created: Washington: U.S. Govt. Print. Off., 1977 [i.e. 1978]
Related Names: United States. Congress. Senate. Committee on Environment and
Public Works. United States. Law, statutes, etc. Federal water pollution control

act. 1978.
Description: iv, 125 p.; 24 cm.
Notes: At head of title: 95th Congress, 1st session. Committee print. "Serial no. 95-12." "Printed for the use of the Senate Committee on Environment and Public Works."
Subjects: Water--Pollution--Law and legislation--United States.
LC Classification: KF3786.A55 C6
Dewey Class No.: 344/.73/0463

The Clean Water Act: 25th anniversary edition / Water Environment Federation.
Cover Title: Clean Water Act, updated for 1997
Published/Created: Alexandria, VA (601 Wythe St., Alexandria 22314-1994): The Federation, 1997.
Related Names: Water Environment Federation.
Description: xxiii, 423 p.; 26 cm.
Subjects: Water--Pollution--Law and legislation--United States. Water quality--United States.
LC Classification: KF3787.122 .A2 1997
Dewey Class No.: 344.73/046343 21

The Clean Water Act: as amended by the Water Quality Act of 1987 / Michael A. Brown, chairman.
Published/Created: New York, N.Y. (810 Seventh Ave., New York 10019): Practising Law Institute, 1987.
Related Names: Brown, Michael A. (Michael Arthur), 1938- Practising Law Institute.
Description: 376 p.: ill.; 22 cm.
Notes: "Prepared for distribution at the The Clean Water Act as amended by the Water Quality Act of 1987 program, May-June 1987"--P. 5. "C4-4178."
Subjects: Water--Pollution--Law and legislation--United States. Water quality--United States.
Series: Litigation and administrative practice series Litigation course handbook series; no. 144
LC Classification: KF3790.Z9 C58 1987
Dewey Class No.: 344.73/046343 347.30446343 19

The Clean Water Act: new directions: a satellite seminar / cosponsored by the Water Environment Federation: and the American Bar Association section of Natural Resources, Energy, and Environmental Law; and the Center for Continuing Legal Education, in cooperation with U. S. Environmental Protection Agency.
Published/Created: [Chicago, IL]: the American Bar Association, 1996.
Related Names: American Bar Association. Section on Natural Resources, Energy, and Environmental Law. Water Environment Federation. Center for Continuing Legal Education (American Bar Association)
Description: [iii], 317 p.: ill., maps; 28 cm.

Notes: "A four hour ABA satelite seminar, Broadcast live- to over 73 locations." -
- Cover. "January 18, 1996." Panels discuss watershed management, effluent
trading, NPDES permits, wet weather problems, and enforcement issues.
Subjects: United States. Federal Water Pollution Control Act. Water--Pollution--
Law and legislation--United States. Water quality management--United States.
LC Classification: KF3790.Z9 C588 1996

The Clean Water Act: the next steps in new directions: May 29, 1997, an ABA
   satellite seminar / co-sponsored by the American Bar Association, Section of
   Natural Resources, Energy, and Environmental Law ... [et al.].
   Published/Created: [Chicago]: American Bar Association, c1997.
   Related Names: American Bar Association. Section of Natural Resources,
   Energy, and Environmental Law.
   Description: 218 p.; 28 cm.
   Subjects: Water--Pollution--Law and legislation--United States.
   LC Classification: KF3790.Z9 C589 1997
   Dewey Class No.: 344.73/046343 21

The State of Texas water quality inventory.
   Edition Information: 10th ed.
   Published/Created: Austin, Tex.: Texas Water Commission, [1990]
   Description: vii, 652 p.: maps (some col.); 28 cm. + 27 col. folded maps.
   Notes: "Pursuant to section 305(b) Federal Clean Water Act." "LP 90-06." "June
   1990."
   Subjects: Water quality--Texas. Water quality management--Texas.
   LC Classification: TD224.T4 S76 1990
   Dewey Class No.: 363.73/942/09764 20

The State of Texas water quality inventory.
   Edition Information: 9th ed.
   Published/Created: Austin, Tex. (P.O. Box 13087, Austin 78711): Texas Water
   Commission, 1988.
   Related Names: Texas Water Commission.
   Description: x, 606, [26] p.: ill. (some col.); 28 cm.
   Notes: "Pursuant to section 305(b) Federal Clean Water Act." "LP 8804."
   Subjects: Water quality--Texas. Water quality management--Texas.
   LC Classification: TD224.T4 S76 1988
   Dewey Class No.: 363.73/942/09764 20

The State of Texas water quality inventory.
   Edition Information: 8th ed.
   Published/Created: Austin, Tex. (P.O. Box 13087, Austin 78711): Texas Water
   Commission, 1986.
   Related Names: Texas Water Commission.
   Description: vii, 584, [30] p.: ill., maps (some col.); 28 cm.

Notes: "Pursuant to section 305 (b) Federal Clean Water Act." "LP 86-07."
Subjects: Water quality--Texas.
LC Classification: TD224.T4 S76 1986
Dewey Class No.: 363.7/3942/09764 19

The status of water quality in Arizona: Clean water act section 305(b) report ...
Published: Phoenix, Ariz.: Arizona Dept. of Environmental Quality, 2000-
Description: v.: ill.; 28 cm. 2000-
Current Frequency: Biennial Continues: Arizona water quality assessment (DLC)
97640149 (OCoLC)27637856
Notes: Title from cover.
Subjects: Water quality management--Arizona--Periodicals.
LC Classification: TD224.A7 W37
Dewey Class No.: 363.7/3942/09791 19

Understanding the Clean Water Act: ALI-ABA CLE TV video for lawyers: study
materials.
Published/Created: Philadelphia, PA (4025 Chestnut St., Philadelphia 19104):
American Law Institute-American Bar Association Committee on Continuing
Professional Education, c1995.
Related Names: American Law Institute-American Bar Association Committee
on Continuing Professional Education.
Description: xiii, 229 p.; 28 cm.
Notes: "Y165." Includes bibliographical references.
Subjects: Water--Pollution--Law and legislation--United States.
LC Classification: KF3790.Z9 U53 1995
Dewey Class No.: 344.73/046343 347.30446343 20

United States. Congress. House. Committee on Merchant Marine and Fisheries.
Subcommittee on Environment and Natural Resources.
Clean water funding: hearing before the Subcommittee on Environment and
Natural Resources of the Committee on Merchant Marine and Fisheries, House of
Representatives, One Hundred Third Congress, first session, on achieving the
objectives of the Clean Water Act, February 18, 1993.
Published/Created: Washington: U.S. G.P.O.: For sale by the U.S. G.P.O., Supt.
of Docs., Congressional Sales Office, 1993.
Description: iii, 222 p.: ill.; 24 cm.
ISBN: 0160409284
Notes: Distributed to some depository libraries in microfiche. Shipping list no.:
93-0303-P. "Serial no. 103-1." Includes bibliographical references (p. 162-169).
Subjects: Water--Pollution--Law and legislation--Water quality management--
United States--Finance. Federal aid to water quality management--United States.
LC Classification: KF27 .M439 1993
Govt. Doc. No.: Y 4.M 53:103-1

United States. Congress. House. Committee on Merchant Marine and Fisheries.
Subcommittee on Environment and Natural Resources.
Clean Water Act reauthorization: hearing before the Subcommittee on
Environment and Natural Resources of the Committee on Merchant Marine and
Fisheries, House of Representatives, One Hundred Third Congress, 1st session ...
Published/Created: Washington: U.S. G.P.O.: For sale by the U.S. G.P.O., Supt.
of Docs., Congressional Sales Office, 1993-1994.
Description: 2 v.: ill., maps; 24 cm.
ISBN: 0160416558
Notes: "March 22, 1994"--Pt. 2. Distributed to some depository libraries in
microfiche. Shipping list no.: 93-0642-P. "Serial no. 103-42"--Pt. 1; "Serial no.
103-105"--Pt. 2. Includes bibliographical references.
Subjects: Sewage disposal--Law and legislation--California--San Diego. Sewage
disposal--California--San Diego--Safety measures. Water--Purification--United
States--Cost of operation. Water quality management--United States--Finance.
LC Classification: KF27 .M439 1993b
Govt. Doc. No.: Y 4.M 53:103-42

United States. Congress. House. Committee on Merchant Marine and Fisheries.
Subcommittee on Fisheries and Wildlife Conservation and the Environment.
National Clean Water Investment Corporation and options for clean water
funding: hearing before the Subcommittee on Fisheries and Wildlife
Conservation and the Environment and the Subcommittee on Oceanography,
Great Lakes, and the Outer Continental Shelf of the Committee on Merchant
Marine and Fisheries, House of Representatives, One Hundred Second Congress,
second session, on the future course of the Federal Clean Water Act ... August 11,
1992.
Published/Created: Washington: U.S. G.P.O.: For sale by the U.S. G.P.O., Supt.
of Docs., Congressional Sales Office, 1992.
Related Names: United States. Congress. House. Committee on Merchant Marine
and Fisheries. Subcommittee on Oceanography, Great Lakes, and the Outer
Continental Shelf.
Description: v, 138 p.: ill.; 24 cm.
ISBN: 0160396123
Notes: Item 1021-B Item 1021-C (MF) Distributed to some depository libraries in
microfiche. Shipping list no.: 93-0100-P. "Serial no. 102-90." Includes
bibliographical references.
Subjects: National Clean Water Investment Corporation (U.S.) Water--Pollution--
Law and legislation--United States. Water quality management--United States--
Finance. Federal aid to water quality management--United States.
LC Classification: KF27 .M447 1992f
Govt. Doc. No.: Y 4.M 53:102-90

United States. Congress. House. Committee on Merchant Marine and Fisheries.
Subcommittee on Fisheries and Wildlife Conservation and the Environment.

Environmental credit projects under Clean Water Act: hearing before the
Subcommittee on Fisheries and Wildlife Conservation and the Environment and
the Subcommittee on Oceanography of the Committee on Merchant Marine and
Fisheries, House of Representatives, One Hundredth Congress, first session, on
H.R. 3411 ... November 4, 1987.
Published/Created: Washington: U.S. G.P.O.: For sale by the Supt. of Docs.,
Congressional Sales Office, U.S. G.P.O., 1988.
Related Names: United States. Congress. House. Committee on Merchant Marine
and Fisheries. Subcommittee on Oceanography.
Description: v, 88 p.; 24 cm.
Notes: Distributed to some depository libraries in microfiche. Shipping list no.:
88-129-P. "Serial no. 100-36." Item 1021-B, 1021-C (microfiche) Includes
bibliographical references.
Subjects: Water--Pollution--Law and legislation--United States. Environmental
law--United States. Federal aid to water quality management--United States.
LC Classification: KF27 .M447 1987h
Dewey Class No.: 344.73/046343 347.30446343 19
Govt. Doc. No.: Y 4.M 53:100-36

United States. Congress. House. Committee on Public Works and Transportation.
    Subcommittee on Investigations and Oversight.
    Administration of Section 404 of the Clean Water Act: hearing before the
    Subcommittee on Investigations and Oversight of the Committee on Public
    Works and Transportation, House of Representatives, One Hundredth Congress,
    second session, September 14, 1988.
    Published/Created: Washington: U.S. G.P.O.: For sale by the Supt. of Docs.,
    Congressional Sales Office, U.S. G.P.O., 1989.
    Description: iv, 545 p.: ill., maps; 24 cm.
    Notes: "100-79." Item 1024-A, 1024-B (microfiche) Bibliography: p. 545.
    Subjects: United States. Army. Corps of Engineers. Wetland conservation--
    United States. Dredging spoil--United States.
    LC Classification: KF27 .P89632 1988i

United States. Congress. House. Committee on Public Works and Transportation.
    Subcommittee on Water Resources and Environment.
    The Water Quality Act of 1994, and issues related to Clean Water Act
    reauthorization (H.R. 3948): hearings before the Subcommittee on Water
    Resources and Environment of the Committee on Public Works and
    Transportation, House of Representatives, One Hundred Third Congress, second
    session, May 24 and 26, 1994.
    Published/Created: Washington: U.S. G.P.O.: For sale by the U.S. G.P.O., Supt.
    of Docs., Congressional Sales Office, 1995.
    Description: cxv, 1777 p.: ill., maps; 24 cm.
    ISBN: 0160465834
    Notes: Distributed to some depository libraries in microfiche. Shipping list no.:

95-0075-P. "103-82." Includes bibliographical references.
Subjects: Water--Pollution--Law and legislation--United States. Federal aid to
water quality management--United States. United States--Appropriations and
expenditures.
LC Classification: KF27 .P8968 1994c
Dewey Class No.: 363.6/1/0973 20
Govt. Doc. No.: Y 4.P 96/11:103-82

United States. Congress. House. Committee on Public Works and Transportation.
Subcommittee on Investigations and Oversight.
Implementation of the Federal Clean Water Act (EPA enforcement of the national
pollution discharge elimination system permit program): hearings before the
Subcommittee on Investigations and Oversight of the Committee on Public
Works and Transportation, House of Representatives, second session, March 7, 8;
September 19, 1984.
Published/Created: Washington: U.S. G.P.O., 1985.
Description: iv, 758 p.: ill., forms; 24 cm.
Notes: Distributed to some depository libraries in microfiche. "98-81." Item
1024-A, 1024-B (microfiche) Includes bibliographical references.
Subjects: Environmental Protection Agency. Water--Pollution--Government
policy--United States.
LC Classification: KF27 .P89632 1984c
Dewey Class No.: 353.0082/325 19
Govt. Doc. No.: Y 4.P 96/11:98-81

United States. Congress. House. Committee on Public Works and Transportation.
Subcommittee on Investigations and Oversight.
Implementation of the Clean Water Act (concerning waiver provisions for
municipal ocean dischargers): hearings before the Subcommittee on
Investigations and Oversight of the Committee on Public Works and
Transportation, House of Representatives, Ninety-seventh Congress, first and
second sessions: September 8, 1981 (Los Angeles, Calif.), February 18, 1982
(Washington, D.C.).
Published/Created: Washington: U.S. G.P.O., 1983.
Description: vii, 1042 p.: ill.; 24 cm.
Notes: "97-84." Includes bibliographies.
Subjects: Refuse and refuse disposal--Waste disposal in the ocean--California.
Refuse and refuse disposal-Waste disposal in the ocean-Law and legislation-U S.
LC Classification: KF27 .P89632 1981h
Dewey Class No.: 353.0082/325 19

United States. Congress. House. Committee on Public Works and Transportation.
Subcommittee on Investigations and Oversight.
Memorandum of agreement between the United States Army Corps of Engineers
and the United States Environmental Protection Agency concerning wetlands

mitigation required under section 404 of the Clean Water Act: hearing before the Subcommittee on Investigations and Oversight of the Committee on Public Works and Transportation, House of Representatives, One Hundred First Congress, second session, February 20, 1990.
Published/Created: Washington [D.C.]: U.S. G.P.O.: For sale by the Supt. of Docs., Congressional Sales Office, U.S. G.P.O., 1990.
Description: iii, 70 p.; 24 cm.
Notes: Distributed to some depository libraries in microfiche. Shipping list no.: 91-003-P. "101-50." Item 1024-A, 1024-B (MF)
Subjects: Army. Corps of Engineers. Environmental Protection Agency. Wetland mitigation--Wetlands--Law and legislation--United States.
LC Classification: KF27 .P89632 1990c
Govt. Doc. No.: Y 4.P 96/11:101-50

United States. Congress. House. Committee on Public Works and Transportation. Subcommittee on Investigations and Oversight.
Implementation of the Federal Clean Water Act: (management of the construction grants program and the Elk Pinch and Malden, West Virginia wastewater treatment projects): hearing before the Subcommittee on Investigations and Oversight of the Committee on Public Works and Transportation, House of Representatives, second session, May 23, 1984.
Published/Created: Washington: U.S. G.P.O., 1985.
Description: iii, 210 p.; 24 cm.
Notes: Distributed to some depository libraries in microfiche. "98-80." Item 1024-A, 1024-B (microfiche) Y 4.P 96/11:98-80
Subjects: Federal aid to water quality management--West Virginia. Water quality management--West Virginia. Water reuse--West Virginia.
LC Classification: KF27 .P89632 1984a
Dewey Class No.: 353.0087/1 19

United States. Congress. House. Committee on Public Works and Transportation. Subcommittee on Investigations and Oversight.
Implementation of the Clean Water Act concerning ocean discharge waivers: (a case study of lawmaking by rulemakers): report / by the Subcommittee on Investigations and Oversight of the Committee on Public Works and Transportation, U.S. House of Representatives.
Published/Created: Washington: U.S. G.P.O., 1983.
Description: iii, 198 p.: ill.; 24 cm.
Notes: At head of title: 97th Congress, 2d session. Committee print. "December 1982." Includes bibliographical references.
Subjects: Refuse and refuse disposal--Waste disposal in the ocean--Administrative procedure--Law and legislation--United States.
LC Classification: KF3786.A55 P85 1983
Dewey Class No.: 353.0082/325 19

United States. Congress. House. Committee on Science and Technology.
Subcommittee on Natural Resources, Agriculture Research, and Environment.
The research needs of the Clean Water Act: hearings before the Subcommittee on
Natural Resources, Agriculture Research, and Environment of the Committee on
Science and Technology, U.S. House of Representatives, Ninety-seventh
Congress, second session, June 8, 10, 1982.
Published/Created: Washington: U.S. G.P.O., 1983.
Description: iii, 662 p.: ill., maps; 24 cm.
Notes: "No. 175." Item 1025-A-1, 1025-A-2 (microfiche) Includes bibliographies.
Subjects: United States. Environmental Protection Agency. Water--Pollution--
Research--United States. Water--Pollution--Law and legislation--United States.
Federal aid to water quality management--United States.
LC Classification: KF27 .S3978 1982h
Dewey Class No.: 344.73/046343/072 347.30446343072 19
Govt. Doc. No.: Y 4.Sci 2:97/175

United States. Congress. House. Committee on Science, Space, and Technology.
Subcommittee on Environment.
Clean Water Act research and monitoring: hearing before the Subcommittee on
Environment of the Committee on Science, Space, and Technology, U.S. House
of Representatives, One Hundred Second Congress, first session, June 5, 1991.
Published/Created: Washington: U.S. G.P.O.: For sale by the U.S. G.P.O., Supt.
of Docs., Congressional Sales Office, 1991.
Description: iii, 321 p.: ill., maps; 24 cm.
ISBN: 0160356989
Notes: Distributed to some depository libraries in microfiche. Shipping list no.:
91-717-P. Item 1025-A-1, 1025-A-2 (MF) "No. 52." Includes bibliographical
references.
Subjects: Water--Pollution--Government policy--United States. Water--Pollution-
-Law and legislation--United States. Water--Pollution--United States--
Measurement. Federal aid to water quality management--United States.
LC Classification: KF27 .S395 1991b
Dewey Class No.: 351.82/325 20
Govt. Doc. No.: Y 4.Sci 2:102/52

United States. Congress. House. Committee on Science, Space, and Technology.
Subcommittee on Technology, Environment, and Aviation.
H.R. 1116, the Clean Water Act Research Amendments of 1993: hearing before
the Subcommittee on Technology, Environment, and Aviation of the Committee
on Science, Space, and Technology, U.S. House of Representatives, One Hundred
Third Congress, first session, September 23, 1993.
Published/Created: Washington: U.S. G.P.O.: For sale by the U.S. G.P.O., Supt.
of Docs., Congressional Sales Office, 1994.
Related Titles: HR 1116, the Clean Water Act Research Amendments of 1993.
Description: v, 172 p.; 24 cm.

ISBN: 0160433886
Notes: Distributed to some depository libraries in microfiche. Shipping list no.:
94-0012-P. "No. 66."
Subjects: Water--Pollution--Law and legislation--United States. Water--Pollution-
-Research--United States. Water quality--Research--United States.
LC Classification: KF27 .S39957 1993u
Govt. Doc. No.: Y 4.SCI 2:103/66

United States. Congress. House. Committee on Transportation and Infrastructure.
Subcommittee on Oversight, Investigations, and Emergency Management.
Total maximum daily load initiatives under the Clean Water Act: hearing before
the Subcommittee on Oversight, Investigations, and Emergency Management of
the Committee on Transportation and Infrastructure, House of Representatives,
One Hundred Sixth Congress, second session, July 27, 2000.
Published/Created: Washington: U.S. G.P.O.: For sale by the U.S. G.P.O., Supt.
of Docs., Congressional Sales Office, 2000 [i.e. 2001]
Description: iii, 77 p.; 23 cm.
ISBN: 0160649668
Notes: Distributed to some depository libraries in microfiche. Shipping list no.:
2001-0162-P. "106-106."
Subjects: United States. Environmental Protection Agency--Rules and practice.
Water--Pollution--Total maximum daily load--United States. Water quality--
United States--Measurement. Water quality management--United States.
LC Classification: KF27 .P89637 2000e
Govt. Doc. No.: Y 4.T 68/2:106-106

United States. Congress. House. Committee on Transportation and Infrastructure.
Subcommittee on Water Resources and Environment.
Governors' perspectives on the Clean Water Act: hearing before the
Subcommittee on Water Resources and Environment of the Committee on
Transportation and Infrastructure, House of Representatives, One Hundred Sixth
Congress, first session, February 23, 1999.
Published/Created: Washington: U.S. G.P.O.: For sale by the U.S. G.P.O., Supt.
of Docs., Congressional Sales Office, 1999.
Description: iii, 56 p.; 24 cm.
ISBN: 0160587654
Notes: Distributed to some depository libraries in microfiche. Shipping list no.:
99-0342-P. "106-12."
Subjects: Water--Pollution--Law and legislation--United States. Water quality--
United States. Federal aid to water quality management--United States.
LC Classification: KF27 .P8968 1999k
Govt. Doc. No.: Y 4.T 68/2:106-12

United States. Congress. Senate. Committee on Appropriations. Subcommittee on
Energy and Water Development.

Issues related to federal wetlands protection program under the Clean Water Act: hearing before a subcommittee of the Committee on Appropriations, United States Senate, One Hundred Third Congress, second session, special hearing.
Published/Created: Washington: U.S. G.P.O.: For sale by the U.S. G.P.O., Supt. of Docs., Congressional Sales Office, 1994.
Description: iii, 105 p.: ill.; 24 cm.
ISBN: 0160460336
Notes: Distributed to some depository libraries in microfiche. Shipping list no.: 94-0368-P. Includes bibliographical references.
Subjects: Wetland conservation--Law and legislation--United States. Wetland conservation--Louisiana. Water--Pollution--Law and legislation--United States.
Series: United States. Congress. Senate. S. hrg.; 103-773.
Variant Series: S. hrg.; 103-773
LC Classification: KF26 .A6469 1994a
Govt. Doc. No.: Y 4.AP 6/2:S.HRG.103-773

United States. Congress. Senate. Committee on Environment and Public Works.
Clean Water Act issues: hearing before the Committee on Environment and Public Works, United States Senate, first session on S. 188 ... S. 669 ... S. 1706 ... October 13, 1999.
Published/Created: Washington: U.S. G.P.O.: For sale by the U.S. G.P.O., Supt. of Docs., Congressional Sales Office, 2000.
Description: iii, 90 p.; 24 cm.
Notes: "Printed for the use of the Committee on Environment and Public Works." Includes bibliographical references.
Subjects: Water--Pollution--Law and legislation--United States. Environmental law--United States.
Series: United States. Congress. Senate. S. hrg.; 106-590.
Variant Series: S. hrg.; 106-590
LC Classification: KF26 .E6 1999h
Govt. Doc. No.: Y 4.P 96/10:S.HRG.106-590

United States. Congress. Senate. Committee on Environment and Public Works. Subcommittee on Environmental Pollution.
Section 404 of the Clean Water Act: hearings before the Subcommittee on Environmental Pollution of the Committee on Environment and Public Works, United States Senate, Ninety-seventh Congress, second session, July 8, 1982, Anchorage, Alaska, July 16, 1982, Washington, D.C.
Published/Created: Washington: U.S. G.P.O., 1982.
Related Titles: Section four hundred four of the Clean Water Act. Section four hundred and four of the Clean Water Act.
Description: vi, 428 p.: ill., maps; 24 cm.
Notes: "Serial no. 97-H65." Item 1045-A, 1045-B (microfiche)
Subjects: Dredging spoil--Law and legislation--Alaska. Wetlands--Law and legislation--Alaska. Dredging spoil--Law and legislation--United States.

Wetlands--Law and legislation--United States. Water--Pollution--Law and legislation--United States.
LC Classification: KF26 .E645 1982h
Dewey Class No.: 344.73/046343 347.30446343 19
Govt. Doc. No.: Y 4.P 96/10:97-H-65

United States. Congress. Senate. Committee on Environment and Public Works. Subcommittee on Environmental Pollution.
A proposal to amend Section 311 of the Clean water act of 1977: hearing before the Subcommittee on Environmental Pollution of the Committee on Environment and Public Works, United States Senate, Ninety-fifth Congress, second session, October 5, 1978.
Published/Created: Washington: U.S. Govt. Print. Off., 1978.
Description: iii, 39 p.; 24 cm.
Notes: "Serial no. 95-H77."
Subjects: Water--Pollution--Law and legislation--United States.
LC Classification: KF26 .E645 1978b
Dewey Class No.: 343/.73/092

United States. Congress. Senate. Committee on Environment and Public Works.
Clean Water Act Amendments: non-point source management program: hearings before the Committee on Environment and Public Works, United States Senate, Ninety-eighth Congress, first session, July 19, 1983--Washington, D.C., August 24, 1983--Moorehead, Minn.
Published/Created: Washington: U.S. G.P.O., 1983.
Description: v, 672 p.: ill., forms, maps; 24 cm.
Notes: Distributed to some depository libraries in microfiche. Item 1045-A, 1045-B (microfiche) Includes bibliographical references.
Subjects: Nonpoint source pollution--Law and legislation--United States. Federal aid to water quality management--United States. Nonpoint source pollution--United States.
Variant Series: S. hrg.; 98-420
LC Classification: KF26 .E6 1983i
Dewey Class No.: 353.0082/325 19
Govt. Doc. No.: Y 4.P 96/10:S.hrg.98-420

United States. Congress. Senate. Committee on Environment and Public Works. Subcommittee on Environmental Pollution.
Clean Water Act amendments of 1982: hearings before the Subcommittee on Environmental Pollution of the Committee on Environment and Public Works, United States Senate, Ninety-seventh Congress, second session, in S. 777 ... S. 2652 ... July 21, 22, 28, and 29, 1982.
Published/Created: Washington: U.S. G.P.O., 1982.
Description: vi, 1373 p.: ill., maps; 24 cm.
Notes: "Serial no. 97-H58." Item 1045-A, 1045-B (microfiche) Includes

bibliographical references.
Subjects: Water--Pollution--Law and legislation--United States.
LC Classification: KF26 .E645 1982d
Dewey Class No.: 344.73/046343 347.30446343 19
Govt. Doc. No.: Y 4.P 96/10:97-H 58

United States. Congress. Senate. Committee on Environment and Public Works.
Coastal water quality issues in Rhode Island: hearing before the Committee on
Environment and Public Works, United States Senate, One Hundred Second
Congress, second session, on reauthorization of the Clean Water Act and the
status of the Narragansett Bay comprehensive conservation and management
plan, April 23, 1992--Providence, RI.
Published/Created: Washington: U.S. G.P.O.: For sale by the U.S. G.P.O., Supt.
of Docs., Congressional Sales Office, 1992.
Description: iii, 115 p.: ill.; 24 cm.
ISBN: 016038818X
Notes: Item 1045-A, 1045-B (MF) Distributed to some depository libraries in
microfiche. Shipping list no.: 92-0469-P.
Subjects: Coastal zone management--Rhode Island--Narragansett Bay. Water
quality management--Rhode Island--Narragansett Bay. Water--Pollution--Rhode
Island--Narragansett Bay.
Series: United States. Congress. Senate. S. hrg.; 102-669.
Variant Series: S. hrg.; 102-669
LC Classification: KF26 .E6 1992b

United States. Congress. Senate. Committee on Environment and Public Works.
Subcommittee on Environmental Protection.
Clean Water Act oversight: hearing before the Subcommittee on Environmental
Protection of the Committee on Environment and Public Works, United States
Senate, One Hundred First Congress, first session, June 16, 1989.
Published/Created: Washington [D.C.]: U.S. G.P.O.: For sale by the Supt. of
Docs., Congressional Sales Office, 1989.
Description: iii, 236 p.; 24 cm.
Notes: Distributed to some depository libraries in microfiche. Shipping list no.:
89-572-P. Item 1045-A, 1045-B (microfiche) Includes bibliographical references.
Subjects: Water--Pollution--Law and legislation--United States. Federal aid to
water quality management--United States.
Series: United States. Congress. Senate. S. hrg.; 101-171.
Variant Series: S. hrg.; 101-171
LC Classification: KF26 .E647 1989l
Dewey Class No.: 353.0082/325 20

United States. Congress. Senate. Committee on Environment and Public Works.
Subcommittee on Environmental Protection.
Implementation of section 404 of the Clean Water Act: hearings before the

Subcommittee on Environmental Protection of the Committee on Environment
and Public Works, United States Senate, One Hundred Second Congress, first
session, June 20; July 10; and November 22, 1991.
Published/Created: Washington: U.S. G.P.O.: For sale by the U.S. G.P.O., Supt.
of Docs., Congressional Sales Office, 1992.
Description: v, 464 p.: ill., maps; 24 cm.
ISBN: 016037538X
Notes: Item 1045-A, 1045-B (MF) Distributed to some depository libraries in
microfiche. Shipping list no.: 92-205-P. Includes bibliographical references.
Subjects: Wetlands--Law and legislation--United States. Dredging spoil--Law and
legislation--United States. Water--Pollution--Law and legislation--United States.
Wetland conservation--Government policy--United States.
Series: United States. Congress. Senate. S. hrg.; 102-450.
Variant Series: S. hrg.; 102-450
LC Classification: KF26 .E647 1991o
NAL Class No.: KF26.E647 1992
Dewey Class No.: 353.0082/326 20
Govt. Doc. No.: Y 4.P 96/10:S.hrg.102-450

United States. Congress. Senate. Committee on Environment and Public Works.
    Subcommittee on Environmental Pollution.
    Oversight hearings on section 404 of the Clean Water Act: hearings before the
    Subcommittee on Environmental Pollution of the Committee on Environment and
    Public Works, United States Senate, 99th Congress, 1st [second] session ....
    Published/Created: Washington: U.S. G.P.O., 1985-<1986 >
    Description: v. <1-2 >: ill.; 23 cm.
    Notes: Hearings held May 21, 1985-<July 31, 1986 > Distributed to some
    depository libraries in microfiche. Shipping list no.: 85-1152-P. Item 1045-A,
    1045-B (microfiche) Includes bibliographical references.
    Subjects: Dredging spoil--Law and legislation--United States. Wetlands--Law and
    legislation--United States. Water--Pollution--Law and legislation--United States.
    Series: United States. Congress. Senate. S. hrg.; 99-278.
    Variant Series: S. hrg.; 99-278
    LC Classification: KF26 .E645 1985g
    Dewey Class No.: 344.73/04626 347.3044626 19
    Govt. Doc. No.: Y 4.P 96/10:S.hrg.99-278

United States. Congress. Senate. Committee on Environment and Public Works.
    Subcommittee on Environmental Pollution.
    Implementation of certain sections of the Clean water act: hearings before the
    Subcommittee on Environmental Pollution of the Committee on Environment and
    Public Works, United States Senate, Ninety-sixth Congress, second session, June
    23, 24, and July 1, 1980.
    Published/Created: Washington: U.S. Govt. Print. Off., 1980.
    Related Titles: Clean water act.

Description: iv, 376 p.: ill.; 24 cm.
Notes: "Serial no. 96-H55." Includes bibliographical references.
Subjects: Wetland conservation--Government policy--United States.
LC Classification: KF26 .E645 1980c
Dewey Class No.: 353.0082/326 19

United States. Congress. Senate. Committee on Environment and Public Works.
Clean Water Act: municipal issues: hearing before the Committee on
Environment and Public Works, United States Senate, One Hundred Fourth
Congress, first session, December 13, 1995.
Published/Created: Washington: U.S. G.P.O.: For sale by the U.S. G.P.O., Supt.
of Docs., Congressional Sales Office, 1996.
Description: iv, 202 p.: ill., maps; 24 cm.
ISBN: 0160529417
Notes: Distributed to some depository libraries in microfiche. Shipping list no.:
96-0333-P. Includes bibliographical references.
Subjects: Water--Pollution--Law and legislation--United States. Liability for
water pollution damages--United States. Tort liability of municipal corporations--
United States. Civil penalties--United States.
Series: United States. Congress. Senate. S. hrg.; 104-518.
Variant Series: S. hrg.; 104-518
LC Classification: KF26 .E6 1996a
Govt. Doc. No.: Y 4.P 96/10:S.HRG.104-518

United States. Congress. Senate. Committee on Environment and Public Works.
Subcommittee on Environmental Pollution.
Amending the Clean Water Act: hearings before the Subcommittee on
Environmental Pollution of the Committee on Environment and Public Works,
United States Senate, Ninety-ninth Congress, first session, on S. 53 ... and S. 652
... March 26, 27, and 28, 1985.
Published/Created: Washington: U.S. G.P.O., 1985.
Description: v, 667 p.: ill., forms; 24 cm.
Notes: Distributed to some depository libraries in microfiche. Item 1045-A, 1045-
B (microfiche) Bibliography: p. 196-197.
Subjects: Water--Pollution--Law and legislation--United States. Sewage disposal
plants--Finance--Law and legislation United States.
Series: United States. Congress. Senate. S. hrg.; 99-64.
Variant Series: S. hrg.; 99-64
LC Classification: KF26 .E645 1985a
Dewey Class No.: 344.73/046343/0262 347.304463430262 19
Govt. Doc. No.: Y 4.P 96/10:S.hrg.99-64

United States. Congress. Senate. Committee on Environment and Public Works.
Subcommittee on Environmental Pollution.
Implementation of the Clean Water Act: hearing before the Subcommittee on

Environmental Pollution of the Committee on Environment and Public Works, United States Senate, Ninety-seventh Congress, second session, February 5, 1982.
Published/Created: Washington: U.S. G.P.O., 1982.
Description: ii, 31 p.; 24 cm.
Notes: "Serial no. 97-H38." Item 1045-A, 1045-B (microfiche)
Subjects: Water--Pollution--Government policy--United States. Sewage disposal--Government policy--United States. Factory and trade waste--Government policy--United States.
LC Classification: KF26 .E645 1982
Dewey Class No.: 353.0082/325 19
Govt. Doc. No.: Y 4.P 96/10:97-H 38

United States. Congress. Senate. Committee on Environment and Public Works. Subcommittee on Clean Water, Fisheries, and Wildlife.
Reauthorization of the Clean Water Act: hearings before the Subcommittee on Clean Water, Fisheries, and Wildlife of the Committee on Environment and Public Works, United States Senate, One Hundred Third Congress, first session, on S. 1114 ... S. 1302 ... June 16, 23; July 1, 14, 27; August 4, 5; and September 15, 1993.
Published/Created: Washington: U.S. G.P.O.: For sale by the U.S. G.P.O., Supt. of Docs., Congressional Sales Office, 1993 [i.e. 1994]
Description: ix, 1702 p.: ill.; 24 cm.
ISBN: 0160433584
Notes: Distributed to some depository libraries in microfiche. Shipping list no.: 94-0020-P. Includes bibliographical references.
Subjects: Water--Pollution--Law and legislation--United States. Water quality management--United States. Wetland conservation--Law and legislation--United States.
Series: United States. Congress. Senate. S. hrg.; 103-328.
Variant Series: S. hrg.; 103-328
LC Classification: KF26 .E63 1993a
Govt. Doc. No.: Y 4.P 96/10:S.HRG.103-328

United States. Congress. Senate. Committee on Environment and Public Works. Subcommittee on Environmental Pollution.
Extending and amending the Clean Water Act: hearings before the Subcommittee on Environmental Pollution of the Committee on Environment and Public Works, United States Senate, Ninety-eighth Congress, first session, on S. 431 ... S. 432 ... April 6, 7, 14, and June 14, 1983.
Published/Created: Washington: U.S. G.P.O., 1983.
Description: iii, 1181 p.; 24 cm.
Notes: Distributed to some depository libraries in microfiche. "Serial no. 98-247." Item 1045-A, 1045-B (microfiche) Includes bibliographical references.
Subjects: Water--Pollution--Law and legislation--United States.
Series: United States. Congress. Senate. S. hrg.; 98-247.

Variant Series: S. hrg.; 98-247
LC Classification: KF26 .E645 1983c
Dewey Class No.: 344.73/046343/0262 347.304463430262 19
Govt. Doc. No.: Y 4.P 96/10:S.hrg.98-247

United States. Congress. Senate. Committee on Environment and Public Works.
The twentieth anniversary of the Clean Water Act: hearing before the Committee
on Environment and Public Works, United States Senate, One Hundred Second
Congress, second session, September 22, 1992.
Published/Created: Washington: U.S. G.P.O.: For sale by the U.S. G.P.O., Supt.
of Docs., Congressional Sales Office, 1992.
Related Titles: 20th anniversary of the Clean Water Act.
Description: iii, 82 p.; 24 cm.
ISBN: 0160394422
Notes: Includes bibliographical references.
Subjects: Water--Pollution--Law and legislation--United States History. Water
quality--United States--History.
Series: United States. Congress. Senate. S. hrg.; 102-842.
Variant Series: S. hrg.; 102-842
LC Classification: KF26 .E6 1992f
Dewey Class No.: 344.73/046343 347.30446343 20

United States. General Accounting Office. RCED.
Clean Water Act: proposed revisions to EPA regulations to clean up polluted
waters / United States General Accounting Office, Resources, Community, and
Economic Development Division.
Published/Created: Washington, D.C. (P.O. Box 37050, Washington, D.C.
20013): The Office, [2000]
Description: 46, [2] p.; 28 cm.
Notes: Title from subject line. "June 21, 2000"--P. [1]. "GAO/RCED-00-206R"--
P. [1]. "B-285593"--P. [1]. Includes bibliographical references.
Additional Form Avail.: Also issued via the Internet.
Subjects: United States. Environmental Protection Agency--Rules and practice--
Evaluation. United States. Environmental Protection Agency--Data processing--
Evaluation. Water quality management--United States. Water--Pollution--Law
and legislation--United States. Water--Pollution--Economic aspects--United
States.
LC Classification: TD223 .U525 2000b
Dewey Class No.: 363.6/1/0973 21

United States.
The Clean Water Act showing changes made by the 1977 amendments (P.L. 95-
217), the 1978 amendments to sections 104 and 311 (P.L. 95-576), and the 1980
amendments (P.L. 96-483).
Published/Created: Washington: U.S. G.P.O., 1980 [i.e. 1981]

Related Names: United States. Congress. Senate. Committee on Environment and
Public Works.
Description: iv, 127 p.; 24 cm.
Notes: At head of title: 96th Congress, 2d session. Committee print. "Printed for
the use of the Senate Committee on Environment and Public Works." "December
1980." "Serial no. 96-18." Item 1045 Includes bibliographical references.
Subjects: Water--Pollution--Law and legislation--United States.
LC Classification: KF3787.122 .A2 1980
Dewey Class No.: 344.73/046343 347.30446343 19
Govt. Doc. No.: Y 4.P 96/10:96-18

United States.
The Clean Water Act: as amended through December 1981.
Uniform Title: [Federal Water Pollution Control Act
Published/Created: Washington: U.S. G.P.O., 1982.
Related Names: United States. Congress. Senate. Committee on Environment and
Public Works.
Description: iv, 132 p.; 24 cm.
Notes: "Printed for the use of the Senate Committee on Environment and Public
Works." "February 1981." "Serial no. 97-8." Item 1045-A, 1045-B (microfiche)
Includes bibliographical references.
Subjects: Water--Pollution--Law and legislation--United States.
LC Classification: KF3787.122 .A2 1982
Dewey Class No.: 344.73/046343/02632 347.3044634302632 19
Govt. Doc. No.: Y 4.P 96/10:97-8

Water quality assessment for the State of Florida: submitted in accordance with the
Federal Clean Water Act, section 305(b).
Published/Created: [Tallahassee, Fla.]: Standards and Monitoring Section, Bureau
of Surface Water Management, Division of Water Management, Dept. of
Environmental Regulation, [1988]
Related Names: Florida. Bureau of Surface Water Management. Standards and
Monitoring Section.
Description: 105 p.: ill. (some col.); 28 cm. + technical appendix.
Notes: "July 1988."
Subjects: Water quality--Florida. Water quality management--Florida.
LC Classification: TD224.F6 W37 1988
Dewey Class No.: 363.73/94/09759 20

Water quality assessment for water years ... / California State Water Resources Board.
Published/Created: [Sacramento]: The Board, 1986-
Related Names: California. State Water Resources Control Board.
Description: v.: ill.; 28 cm. 1984 & 1985-
Current Frequency: Biennial
Continues: Water quality inventory for water years (DLC) 88658003

(OCoLC)11515449
Continued by: Water quality assessment (Sacramento, Calif.) (DLC)sn 93017093
(OCoLC)27696609
Notes: "Prepared in fulfillment of U.S. Environmental Protection Agency
requirements of Section 305(b) Public Law 92-500 as amended by the Clean
Water Act of 1977 P.L. 95-217." SERBIB/SERLOC merged record
Subjects: Water quality--California--Periodicals. Water--Pollution--California--
Periodicals.
Series: Water quality monitoring report
LC Classification: TD224.C3 C28c
Dewey Class No.: 363.73/942/09794 20

Zalewski, Ann Marie.
State revolving fund: changes to the Federal Clean Water Act, construction grants
program for wastewater treatment plants / prepared by Department of Fiscal
Services.
Edition Information: Rev. Oct. 1987.
Published/Created: [Annapolis, Md.] (90 State Circle, Annapolis 21401-1991):
The Department, [1987]
Related Names: Maryland. General Assembly. Dept. of Fiscal Services.
Description: ii, 223 p.: ill.; 28 cm.
Subjects: United States. Federal Water Pollution Control Act. Sewage disposal
plants--Maryland--Design and construction Finance. Water quality management--
Maryland--Finance. Federal aid to water quality management--United States.
Federal aid to water quality management--Maryland.
LC Classification: HD4479.M3 Z35 1987
Dewey Class No.: 338.4/36283/09752 19

INDEX